Male

Sexual

Fantasies

SIMON & SCHUSTER

Bob Berkowitz

His
Secret
Life

SIMON & SCHUSTER
Rockefeller Center
1230 Avenue of the Americas
New York, NY 10020

Copyright © 1997 by Bob Berkowitz
All rights reserved, including the right of reproduction
in whole or in part in any form.

SIMON & SCHUSTER and colophon are registered trademarks
of Simon & Schuster Inc.

Designed by Brian Mulligan

Manufactured in the United States of America

10 9 8 7 6 5 4 3 2 1

Library of Congress Cataloging-in-Publication Data

Berkowitz, Bob.
His secret life : male sexual fantasies / Bob Berkowitz.
p.   cm.
1. Men—Sexual behavior. 2. Sexual fantasies. I. Title.
HQ29.B476 1997
306.7'081—dc21   97-2258   CIP
ISBN 0-684-81103-0

Acknowledgments

First and foremost, my deepest thanks to all the men who with great candor and courage opened up a secret side of themselves. My collaborator Roger Gittines once again proved that he is not only a wonderful writer but a great friend as well. Much thanks to Judith Regan who encouraged me to write this book. My editor, Laurie Bernstein, picked up this project mid-way through. Nevertheless, she gave it the love, understanding, insight, and helpful criticism as if it were hers from day one. Mona Tanner did an outstanding job in gathering many of the fantasies. Kudos and gratitude also go to Hope Murray, Gloria Brame, and Elaine Steffek. And as always, my agent Margret McBride was always there for me. And special thanks to Kim Sauer for her very helpful editorial guidance. I know I'm leaving out some people, so please know that in my heart, you have my thanks.

To Susan. The love of my life, the supporter of my dreams.

Contents

Part III Beyond Ground Zero

Part IV Other Options

Introduction:
A New Perspective
on Male Sexuality

This is a book not only about his secret life, but also about his *real* life. I'm convinced, both as a journalist and as a man, that by examining the context and texture of male sexual fantasies—*his secret life*—we can come to a better understanding of who he is, what he wants and why he does what he does.

As with the *Yeti,* "Big Foot," rumors of male sexual fantasies have abounded for ages, but only rarely have there been reasonably reliable sightings. Now, for reasons we can only theorize about (and I will in a moment), something happened and men, here and there, have started talking about their sexual fantasies.

At first, it didn't seem like a big deal. But it was. One of the doorways that leads directly into the inner recesses of the male labyrinth, one that had always been locked, barred and boarded up, was suddenly being pried open. The territory now awaits exploration. In the pages ahead, I'll take you across the threshold into the terrain of male sexual fantasy where you'll gain a whole new perspective on men and male sexuality.

Until recently, most male sexual fantasies existed either under a rock, as pornography, or in filing cabinets, as clinical studies. As such, they weren't terribly reliable or helpful to the average person. Did "normal" men—please note the quotation marks—share the same interests and desires? There was no way to know. "Normal" men weren't speaking up.

Now they are.

While each male fantasy is a unique landscape unto itself, there are patterns, clusters of themes, similar chords and points of emphasis that can help explain and illuminate the secret life of men. Next to asking direct questions, getting back direct answers and engaging in an honest dialogue, exploring sexual fantasies is the best way to reach layers of important information and knowledge that are otherwise unavailable.

So why not ask the direct questions?

I have—and so have you. Getting the answers is the problem. We all know by this point that men speak another language. In my first book, *What Men Won't Tell You but Women Need to Know,* published in 1990, I half-seriously suggested that women should enroll in "Boylitz" to learn the lingo. If there were such a language school, I believe that one of the things it would teach is the ability to read "sign" language. Sexual fantasies are not just signs—they are huge billboards.

Men use these billboards to visualize—and the visual is extremely important to men sexually—their emotional and physical needs. What they wouldn't dare tell another person, they'll project up onto the billboard to arouse, satisfy and entertain themselves.

What you'll discover as you read on is that while the images may be graphic and even shocking, it is the subtext of the fantasy that is all-important. Helping you learn to read the hidden meaning and to translate it into actions that will benefit both men and women is the service this book offers its readers.

• • •

I promised to give you my theory about why men are now being more candid about their sexual fantasies and I will do so here briefly: the O-word. Sometime in the early 1970s, or perhaps in the 1960s, feminist thinkers started writing about the orgasm—the forbidden O-word. They introduced women—and men—to concepts of sexuality that had never before been touched by the mass media.

Women got it. They took to this openness about sex, sexuality and their own bodies. They gathered up the information and turned that knowledge into power. I'm talking not only about political power, but also about the power to take charge of their own sexuality and that all-important, always illusive inner self that had been subordinated to socially dictated roles—the "good girl," "the mommy track," "the little woman."

After twenty or twenty-five years, men are now finally getting it too. They are still uneasy when it comes to talking about sex face-to-face or discussing relationships, but thanks to the example set by women they are beginning to ease into the process and give it a try.

I see the sexual fantasies gathered here from roughly five hundred men as evidence that the "Testosterone Curtain" is beginning to come down, and like the Iron Curtain it may soon be totally gone. I really didn't have to search for these male sexual fantasies. Friends, acquaintances, coworkers, friends of friends and men I've met as I've traveled the country willingly supplied the fantasies. The selection was unscientific and random. Not one of them—to my surprise—was bashful about sharing the intimate details of his fantasies. I've changed their names and, in several cases, occupations and hometowns to protect privacy. Some of the fantasies have been edited for length or grammar.

In addition to the O-word, the L-word, *look,* is involved in all of this. As former host of *Real Personal* on CNBC, I was impressed and, frankly, amazed at the utter candor exhibited by our guests when it came to revealing their sexual experiences, innermost feelings and fantasies so that others might look. They seemed to gain strength and confidence from revealing their secret lives to the camera. Our millions of viewers also benefited in equal measure. The frightening isolation and uncertainty that many people feel about their sexuality was broken. They could see a little of themselves on the TV screen each night.

This book will show you even more. In *What Men Won't Tell You but Women Need to Know,* I told readers that, in fact, men won't tell you the most important things, and that it's necessary to become something of a detective. Here, with encouragement from me and the cooperation of many men, they do open up and they do spill their guts. Some of it's quite shocking. A lot of it's extremely erotically stimulating. Some of it's kinky and loopy and fun. All of it is illuminating.

But hold on. Isn't it voyeurism to look so closely at another's secret life? Yes, probably.

And so what?

Looking is fun. Men do plenty of looking, as you'll discover in the pages ahead. Looking is a turn-on.

And another L-word is crucial: learning. Looking is integral to the process of learning. This voyage into the enchanted territories of male fantasy is above all else a voyage of discovery.

The more we know about our own secret lives and each other's the better. How else does a man come to terms with the supercharged emotions, mental images and physical desires that are bombarding him day and night? Turning away, tuning out accomplishes nothing. How else can women ever discover who these men are and what it's like for the men with whom they must share a small planet—not to mention beds, businesses and all the other sweet and sour stuff of everyday existence?

I started this introduction by saying this book is about his *real* life; I'll end by amending that: It's about *our real lives.*

Part I

Who's in Control?

One

Secrets Shared: The Sexually Confident Woman

As a former network White House correspondent and congressional reporter, I believe in putting what journalists call "the lead" where it belongs—at the beginning of the story. In this case, the lead is good news for both men and women. And here it is: There are strong indications that at least one of the defining characteristics of male sexuality is beginning to change, and that change could eventually lead to an end of sex as we know it.

I hope that got your attention. I'm serious. An end to sex as we know it.

I'll bet you're thinking. "If that's the good news, I just can't wait to hear the bad!"

But if I'm right, these early indications are that we are in for some changes that will make our sex lives better than ever.

When I first started researching and writing this book my working assumption was that erotic fantasies would provide a window through which we could observe important aspects of male sexuality. I was right, but early in the process I made an unexpected discovery that amazed me.

Many of the fantasies that men shared with me—only the themes of the ménage à trois and group sex occurred more often—involved physical intimacy with women who were about as far from the stereotypical passive, semireluctant partner as you could get. These fantasies and those women were hot.

At first, the fantasies seemed like more of the same old thing. Men just want to get laid—or so they've always assured us—and dreaming of steamy sex with an Olympic gold medal sexual athlete fits the image. Yet, I actually saw there was more involved than a carnal triathlon. A pattern soon emerged, and men were telling me about fantasies that involved women who were totally comfortable with sex. They enjoyed it, knew what buttons to push (and what to do to have theirs pushed) and didn't pretend otherwise.

And guess what? These guys love the new order of things. Nobody fantasizes about stuff that he or she really dislikes. Nightmares are another thing entirely. The process of dreaming while asleep is a separate subject, which I'm not addressing. Fantasies, however, if nothing else, are forms of harmless recreation or no-fault wish fulfillment. Reality gives us more than enough hard knocks, disappointments and headaches. There's no need to fantasize about those.

What we're dealing with in our fantasy life is a glimpse of ideal sexual scenarios, including some that would have no real-life appeal whatsoever. The ideal does not have to be real and it is not necessarily the one and only ideal, but something that has powerful appeal. And what's so appealing? Great sex is one obvious answer. Another is a desire to step clear of the constraints, the responsibilities and the liabilities of a traditional sexual role that requires men to be the central actors in sexual encounters.

By day, in the boardroom, what the world could be seeing is a powerful, decisive, take-no-prisoners kind of guy. By night in the bed-room, he's a different man—or wants to be. Instead of 100 percent con-trol, he fantasizes about a woman with whom he can share or to whom he can relinquish the power and authority he wields from nine to five.

This shift away from unquestioned male sexual predominance is of great importance. All human behavior patterns are subject to change—some more than others. But sexual behavior patterns are among the most stable. A shift, even in the form of fantasy, in those roles is a big deal.

Roles are the products of generations of custom, habit, practical ne-cessity, convenience, folklore, prejudice, taste and dumb ideas. Along the way, men got to sit up front in the cab of the engine and drive the erotic train; women were stuck with being passengers. No matter whether it's right or wrong, it happened, and we were all railroaded.

The forms taken by this status quo have many variations, ranging from "Me Tarzan, You Jane," to "My place or yours?" Men are ex-pected to take charge of the sexual process and women are supposed to relinquish this function and pretend that the arrangement is just fine with them.

Not all men relish that assigned role and the same is certainly true for women.

What is so illuminating about sexual fantasies, no matter what the theme, is that they are a means of escaping these roles. Without having to actually defy conventional expectations and attitudes, men and women, in the privacy of their own heads, are able to counterbalance sexual assignments that they find constricting and unsatisfying. Even if the fantasy is never acted out—and probably it won't be—it is still an important sexual safety valve and a means of improving the quality of an unfulfilling sex life.

I think these fantasies are telling us that contemporary men are now buying into sexual equality in ways that their fathers and grandfathers would never have accepted and, certainly, would never have expressed openly. A woman who is confident of her sexuality is no longer a threatening harridan bent on robbing men of their masculinity. She's more of a partner than ever before, one who shares many of the same sensual desires and has the right to express them. In other words, the "nice girl–bad girl" foolishness is losing its power to beguile men into believing in a false and destructive sexual double standard.

These fantasies of sexually confident women are reflections of the dawning change in our sexuality and are also a means of furthering that change.

I ran my observations past Doctor June M. Reinisch, the former director of the Kinsey Institute. In her view, men have probably always had the confident-woman fantasy, but what's significant is that they have not been willing to admit it and freely articulate it until now.

To me, that amounts to even better news. The presence over time of the fantasies confirms the presumption of their importance as ideal sexual scenarios. But the fantasies were too dangerous, too threatening to bring out in the open. By finally acknowledging them, men are moving away from denying or suppressing the ideal and moving toward its possible fulfillment.

And I blame women for this momentous shift. But blame is hardly the right word. Let's call it giving credit where credit is due.

The birth control pill and the civil rights and equal rights movements allowed women to examine their own sexual identities and to take action to alter what they didn't like. This seemed to be a sex-specific process. Women changed, men stayed the same. There were inevitable conflicts as a result, and male bashing became a national and international sport.

Finally, after thirty-five or forty years, men have started their own examination of sexual roles and are taking the first tentative steps—via fantasy, at least—toward making changes.

What are the consequences likely to be? In the future—who knows how long—I'd like to hope that men and women would be free, in terms of both their psyches and societal norms, to fully explore their sexuality without regard to roles. If he wants to be aggressive on Monday and passive on Tuesday, and if that works for her—great. Both partners are *full* partners with the right to say yes or no, make suggestions and offer alternatives without feeling that his masculinity is threatened or her personal freedom and femininity compromised.

And now for the bad news. In our case—yours and mine, as author and reader—the fantasies can indeed tell us a lot about the composition of male sexuality, the part that exists independently of prescribed roles. We can see what's going on backstage. And yet, fantasies may also tell us nothing more than he likes to think about having his clothes torn off by a gorgeous redhead. End of story.

Either way, we end up knowing more about him through this aspect of his secret life than we would otherwise be privy to. Less is not more when it comes to understanding our sexuality. More is more. In this case, quantity almost certainly affects quality.

The unexamined sex life is not worth living—and I'm only half kidding.

I believe that lovers should—and must—talk about sex with each other. Why shouldn't they? We talk about other pleasures—food, wine, music, vacations. The pleasure is enhanced and so is our understanding of the experience. The same is true of sex, but conflicts and ambivalence about the propriety of articulating our sexual needs and desires draw a curtain of silence across the subject for many people.

In addition, men have traditionally been reluctant to share their fantasies with their sexual partners, particularly if traditional sexual roles are being challenged. Potentially, it exposes them to ridicule and rejection. There are real concerns that if a man tells his wife about fantasies that are at variance with their actual sex lives as a couple it will harm the relationship. This book is a way around that obstacle.

To speak directly to my female readers: Instead of your lover telling you that he fantasizes about women who are completely comfortable with sex, the men in this chapter can say it for him.

And now, equal time for male readers: The guys in this chapter and the rest of the book are just like you and me. Their penises are not subject to recall because they dared reveal their fantasies or to enjoy them for what they are—pure pleasure.

I believe this is liberating information for both men and women. He can see that he is not alone or out of the "man" stream. We have enough to feel guilty about. Feeling guilty about fantasies is a bit much! Save guilt for reality.

For women, this information can provide an opportunity for reevaluating the sexual roles that have been assigned to them. She may see that he is as frustrated with those roles as she is.

As the former host of CNBC's *Real Personal* I received a lot of mail. At one point, I got a letter from a Roman Catholic priest who was a regular viewer and said he enjoyed the programs. He went on to add, however, that one night he was wondering if all the openness about sex doesn't actually rob it of its mystery. He included his phone number and I immediately called him because I wanted to tell him—and I did—that's the point! There's too much mystery about sex.

Let's go to the fantasies. Notice the similarities in style. They tend to be written in the first person present tense. Most read like play-by-play descriptions of actual events, which reflects just how "real" the fantasies are to the men who have shared them with us.

In many cases, the choice of words comes out of the same grab bag of erotic phraseology that's been the inspiration for what I call the literature of dripping loins and throbbing shafts. Some of it grates on me, too. But keep it in perspective.

By now, all of us know about uncommunicative men. Without subscribing to the stereotype, I have to say that men are so unaccustomed to talking about their secret lives that they frequently fall back on what they've read in the more explicit men's magazines. It's not surprising, in a way. How does one learn to talk about sex, or any other subject, for that matter? Imitation, initially. But when it comes to sex there aren't many role models. Dad wasn't much help. Hence, it's the poetry and prose of *Penthouse* and *Playboy* that set the standard.

As I said—let's go to the fantasies.

High Tide

"Lonnie" is twenty-four and lives in New Jersey. He's a sales assistant selling time to TV network affiliates. "Lonnie" is single. In fact, when we spoke to him, he had just been dumped by his girlfriend of one year, who found out he was unfaithful one night during the beginning stages of their relationship. He told us he is doing everything in his power to win her back. And apparently that includes fantasizing.

> *I'm* on an island with this girl who has just dumped me. In my fantasy, she still loves me. Always, it's nighttime and we are taking a walk on the beach trying to find a nice spot to lie down. We place a blanket on the slope of a small dune, and I take out some wine and peaches and cream from the basket I brought with us. We start to drink the wine and feed each other peaches . . . I pull up her T-shirt and start to kiss her warm stomach.
>
> I raise the shirt over her head and take it off, touching and kissing her breasts at the same time. I put some peaches and cream on her stomach and begin to eat it off of her . . .

letting the cream run down her thighs and licking it all up. I put my tongue inside of her and she tastes so sweet. Her moaning is making me crazy, and I'm touching myself as my tongue slowly undulates inside of her. She pulls me up and begins to tear off my clothes. She lifts the bottle of wine and pours it on me, and starting at my navel, as though it were a tiny cup, sips and licks and drinks me all over. With all of the stickiness we decide to take a swim. We get in the water and she wraps her legs around me, floating on her back and pulling me inside her. The pressure of the water makes my penetration even more difficult, and I'm driving it in as much as I can.

We're creating waves in the ocean, and as water swirls around us it glistens with pinpoints of moonlight, like scattered and floating diamonds. She breaks away from me and swims out and away from the beach for twenty or thirty yards. I stand watching, slowly stroking myself. She turns and swims back, passing me, gliding into the shallows on her belly, head out of the water, resting on her arms as though she's sleeping. I penetrate her from behind . . . the particles of sand on my penis are giving her a harsh sensation and making me even more and more aroused. My body begins to tremble and shake, and I pull in close as I come inside of her. Gentle, foaming waves break over us.

On Deck

"Cliff," thirty-six, lives in Florida. He's a CPA for a regional accounting firm, single and, as he puts it, "fully available."

It's a full moon out, complemented by a nice brisk evening. This girl, "M," and I are on a boat, heading out to the ocean. After a short ride, we decide to anchor in a little quaint spot.

We sit in the front of the boat and sip champagne while we are gazing at the stars. A few glasses of champagne get us in the mood for a little slow dancing and kissing. I start to kiss her neck, her shoulders . . . I turn her round and wrap my arms around her waist and start to kiss her back. She takes my hand and leads me to the cushions on the deck. My hands move down her face and start to caress the outline of her breasts.

I unzip the back of her dress and slowly slip it off. She unbuttons my shirt and starts to kiss my chest. We roll around on the cushions . . . touching, licking, sucking. I roll over on top of her and lower myself down onto her vagina and put my tongue inside her, moving it around, probing her walls. As I flicker my tongue inside her, she arches her back and lets go completely until her juices pour out. I pull myself up and she comes and puts her arms around me and pushes me down. She lowers her mouth onto my penis going in and out, and stroking me up and down.

As I'm about to explode, I lift her up and put her right down onto me. As she rocks back and forth, she leans forward and I suck on her nipples and get smacked in the face with her breasts. I lift her up again and this time I turn her around and bring her legs close together to resist my penetration. I force my way into her, pulling her hips harder and harder toward me for an arousing impact.

I'm getting harder and harder as my balls slap her in the behind. After a few more moments, we indulge in simultaneous orgasm as our bodies shake and expel all our juices.

"Cliff" offered us a second fantasy. This one is land-based but starts at poolside.

I'm at this pool party in a big country house. There are just tons of people walking half-naked all over the place. After a day of swimming in the pool, and with signs of night on the way, I decide to go into the house and change into jeans. I walk in and go up to the second floor where I see a door that's slightly ajar. I immediately head for that one. As I approach I hear noises . . . a girl is moaning . . . I look inside and see that she is masturbating. She has a sexy bathing suit on and her hand is up in her panties.

I watch her in a way that she doesn't know that I am watching. Finally, I catch her eye. She starts to masturbate harder and faster when she sees that I'm watching. My hard-on, at this point, is sticking straight out of my boxers.

I can tell that she is not the aggressive type but will be very receptive. I walk over to her to initiate. I climb on the bed and slowly lower my face where her hand is between her legs. I move her panties to one side and stick my tongue in. At the same time, I'm dental flossing her with the crotch part of her panties. I slide them back and forth. After a few moments of this and some nipple stimulation . . . I bring her to the brink and I stop.

I pull her panties down, slide myself inside, wrap my arms around her and flip on the bed. She is now on top of me, moving back and forth and pinching and fondling her nipples. Her cries and moans make me so aroused . . . I grab her hips and say, "Fuck me!" With my command her actions are almost simultaneous. She starts riding me faster than a jockey would at Belmont race track. It's not enough. I need deeper penetration. I sit up and lift her and turn her around. I slide myself in from the rear, and slide it in and out, in and out, until, needless to say, I can't take it anymore and I wake up.

• • •

I'm going to refrain from interrupting too much during the fantasies to avoid intruding or sounding like a play-by-play announcer. They really do speak for themselves. But I do want to make an observation here that holds pretty much true throughout the book. The similarity of theme and the quality of—dare I say it?—innocence is striking. In addition, these fantasies are all action and little or no dialogue.

What that suggests to me is that while some men may fantasize about moonlight and sailboats and other "romantic" props that might be associated more (correctly or incorrectly) with the female imagination, conversation appears not to be a vital component of ideal male sexual scenarios.

That doesn't come as a surprise to me and, I suspect, won't surprise many women. But it does confirm practical experience and indicate that whatever frustration you may be having in this regard is not uncommon.

Snowplow

"Mark" is a twenty-seven-year-old vice-president of an automotive company in New Castle, Delaware. He told us, "I've been seeing someone for approximately seven months, although I wonder if she realizes it. What I mean is that the relationship is a bit one-sided. I'm completely in, and she's there for the ride . . . I think. I hope she proves me wrong."

> We're on a vacation in Aspen, Colorado . . . me and the girl I'm seeing. For the purposes of this fantasy I will refer to her as "A." We've just spent the day skiing and we're going back to our chalet to get out of our heavy ski clothes.

Our chalet has big bay windows that overlook the whole town and on our way up, we can see that the fireplace is already going. We head inside and take off each other's gear. She helps me with my ski pants, I help her with the tight sweater she's wearing; we undress until there's nothing left.

We lie naked by the fireplace, surveying one another, drinking wine. We indulge in the little picnic that we'd prepared earlier that morning. I feed her crackers with pieces of caviar on them. She takes my fingers into her mouth, along with the food, as a prelude to what is to come. She dips strawberries into the wine and feeds them to me, licking off the juices that dribble down my chin. We start to get closer . . . kissing, teasing one another with slow foreplay. I begin tickling her breasts, nibbling on her neck and moving my hands up and down her body in exploration. I lie on my back and she comes on top of me, sliding against my penis but not allowing me to go in. She keeps rubbing her vagina against my hard-on. I stare into A's eyes and say "Please." She holds my penis at the base straight up, gets up and sits right down on me. She begins to grind her hips. I put my hands up to her nipples and start to twist them.

She's riding me faster. I keep twisting and turning her nipples . . . she moves faster. I take her full breasts into my hands and begin molding them, shaping them, squeezing them . . . she's swinging from side to side and then rocking forward and back, almost lunging . . . I pull up hard with my hips and she puts her arms around me. There are a final few thrusts, and then we tremble and collapse in each other's arms.

A Special Angel

"Brian" is fifty-four, an accountant from Chicago, Illinois. He told us, "I'm single. Did I tell you I'm available and looking?"

My fantasies don't revolve around particular settings. So let's just say that I'm somewhere . . . anywhere. I'm with a strikingly gorgeous girl in some sort of formal dress. Actually, she's in a long white, soft gown that is transparent and flowing . . . she looks like an angel and is very virginlike.

She doesn't speak or ask any questions and only follows my orders; I tell her, "Take off your gown." She stares into my eyes innocently and slowly removes it over her head. As she takes it off, I see her piece by piece, from her thighs to her pussy (she has no underwear on), to her hips and tiny waist, her breasts and shoulders. She's a beautiful sight. "Come here. I want to touch you." She slowly moves toward me, never once removing her eyes from mine. I take her index finger, kiss the tip and put it inside her vagina as she snuggles into my arms. I slide my hand between her thighs and also slip my fingers into her. She pushes her hips toward my fingers so that I can penetrate deeper and deeper. I pull my fingers out and say, "Now undress me. But very slowly."

She starts to unbutton my shirt, kissing each chest hair as it's exposed. Her tongue and breath are warm and moist on my skin. She moves her hands down and unzips me, pulling my pants down. She grinds against my body, feeling my hardness. She pulls down my boxers; my penis is standing straight up. She lowers herself and puts her mouth to it. She takes me in and out between her lips, slowly, seductively and sensually. My hard-on is growing in her mouth. I lie down and bring her on top of me. "Now fuck me," I tell her. She begins to rock back and forth with determination, riding me like a child rides a pony. I grab her waist and shake her wildly till her breasts are smacking up and down violently. I twist and turn her nipples, and she begins to move faster and faster, and when I reach the brink of pleasure and come inside of her she falls back down onto my chest.

It doesn't take a lot of deep analysis to spot the recurring confident-woman theme in these fantasies. In these cases, the women did not have to be persuaded, cajoled or coerced into sex. They took to it naturally and enthusiastically. Even "Brian's" scenario features a willing and eager partner, notwithstanding his statement that she "only follows my orders."

I'm struck, as well, by the overtly romantic settings and touches: a deserted beach, moonlight, a sailboat, the mountains, a pool party at a country hideaway, and an angelic woman in a long white gown. It's as though "Lonnie," "Cliff," "Mark" and "Brian" were tapping into a set of deep sexual archetypes and discovering the usual "hearts and flowers" along with the unusual dynamic of sexual power sharing.

They are updating existing erotic imagery by adding their own needs and desires. To me, that's terrific. There's no reason why sexual roles have to be frozen in time. What works today—or worked a century ago—may be completely dysfunctional in twenty or thirty years. It seems, though, that moonlight and beaches have endurance, and adjusting the script gives these fantasies continued erotic energy.

Now, from the standpoint of fantasy as wish fulfillment, I'd say that the romantic trappings also speak to an interest in removing sex from a humdrum routine setting. wouldn't we all like to make love in front of a cozy fire in a ski chalet in Aspen? Unfortunately, that's not possible for everyone. What is possible is candlelight, music and other flourishes that can give sex a special magic that is too often lacking in many relationships.

Another point: The men and women in the fantasies above get equal billing. They provide pleasure and receive it. That essential give-and-take is where the equality is based. This sex is not one-sided, which may come as a surprise. Fantasies are so personal and private, it would seem they give the man involved (or the woman who fantasizes) the right to have it all. But here, that's not it. The willingness to go "halfsies" comes through load and clear.

The split may not be a strict fifty-fifty every time a couple makes love. Tonight he may want to be more passive and let her control the action; tomorrow that could change. To me, that sounds totally natural and far more interesting than more one-sided relationships.

Some psychologists argue that men are talking a good game about sharing control and power but revert to the traditional "me first" sexual role outside their fantasies. By fantasizing about giving up control, they get a certain kick but then don't have to take the risk of going through with it in reality.

I'm not as skeptical. Just by being willing to talk about these power-sharing fantasies, men are already going well beyond the comfort zone bequeathed to them by their fathers and grandfathers. When a fantasy recurs again and again, it is connecting to a person's emotional grid-work, both receiving juice and generating it. The fantasy is like a post-card a man sends to himself. It says, "Wish you were here."

The chances are good that eventually he'll make the trip—not necessarily by acting out the specifics of the fantasy but by moving toward the themes it expresses.

Two

Secrets Relinquished: Women Who Initiate Sex

Sex is simple. Two consenting adults get together and they ... You know the story.

What isn't simple is the emotional underpinning of this otherwise straightforward biological function and act of physical intimacy.

Men have a variety of techniques for dealing with the complications that accompany the process of copulation. Women do too, but somebody else can write that book. The old standby for men when emotions and hormones start intermingling is to shove the whole subject aside. They try not to think about it.

But that doesn't work all that well because men think about sex a lot. More than they think about the Second Law of Thermodynamics or Chaos Theory.

Much more. Yes, I think I can make that statement without getting into serious trouble.

To avoid nervous breakdowns, the mother of all male rationales for sexual conduct and misconduct was devised: "My penis made me do it." There's no need to go any farther. Or that's what we're supposed to believe.

A working variation, the one I referred to in the last chapter, is "Men just want to get laid"—which is true and, therefore, seems like the definitive last word.

But the contents and the contexts of many of the fantasies that we gathered for this book suggest that men don't believe that deep down. While their sex drive is a strong one, it does not wipe out emotional conflicts and tension. Fantasies are a way to deal with these sore points and, ideally, heal them and transform them into sources of strength and pleasure.

The theme of the sexually confident woman, which we've been examining, is paired with another theme—joined at the hip really—that will be addressed in this chapter. As I sorted through my compilation of fantasies, it hit me that two distinct types of sexually confident women are rocking and rolling and romping in the minds of many men. One of them isn't about to swoon when it comes to sex. She enjoys it and is ready, willing and able to partake. The other is all of that and more. She's a sexual leader, not a follower. She takes the sexual initiative and keeps it.

Now, we're talking big-time emotional conflict and tension. The "Book"—the Book of Roles—says men do the initiating. Sharing power and control is one thing. Giving it up is an entirely different matter. It pulls the rug out from under a set of traditional attitudes about male-female sexual roles that are central to defining a man's identity and purpose.

The power to initiate and control sexual relations is perhaps the paramount male prerogative. It's way ahead of keeping the checkbook, selecting a new car or leaving the toilet seat up. I'm being flippant because I don't want to slip over into heavy-duty sociology. But a lot of important stuff has always hinged on who's in charge of the on-off switch of sexual power.

You're probably as uneasy as I am about introducing the concept of power into the bedroom. Power and sex seem fundamentally incompatible—or should be—at least in terms of love and sharing. But one classic definition of power is relevant: power is a matter of *who does what to whom.*

From that perspective, men traditionally exercised sexual power. They have been ordained by society (some would say "ordained by themselves") as the doer—and women are who they do.

Crude. And I suspect this blatant casting of sexual inferiors and superiors has always been the source of deep misgivings on the part of women as well as men about sexual roles and about who they are as individuals.

And that's why the desire to share power (if that's what the fantasies actually confirm in Chapter One), combined with this chapter's indications of a desire to go even further to relinquish the power to initiate sex and to control the ensuing play, represents a potential major reordering of the sexual dynamic.

As a longtime observer of the political scene, I know that power is never relinquished willingly until the burdens outweigh the benefits.

"My penis made me do it" is a great cop-out. What doesn't it excuse? But the burden of casual, no-fault sex in a civilized age is that before men "do" women they must ask first. Women, consequently, have the right to say no. That negative capability—with all of its positive benefits—is what haunts many men.

The word is "rejection." Men aren't well programmed for it. Not by habit, social custom or nature.

This, then, is the burden that outweighs the benefit. Rejection hurts. A lot.

Rejection does more than damage egos, however. Sexual rejection strikes hard at the core of a man's self-identity. I'm not only talking about being brushed off at singles bar, although that's painful. The larger issue is sexual inadequacy, and it arises more often in the interplay between couples than many women realize. A man needs to see himself as an effective, desirable lover. The truth—whether he is or he isn't—is radioactive.

To protect himself, there is an elaborate, lead-shielded armature that ranges from promiscuity—"I'll screw anything in a skirt and damn the consequences"—to abstinence.

Fear of rejection, fear of confronting even the smallest hints of sexual inadequacy, are key elements of the emotional subtext of male sexuality. They work their way into the contents of fantasies in subtle and dramatic ways. The confident-woman theme not only touches on the issue of changing roles and power sharing, but also addresses these questions of rejection and inadequacy. Fantasy women never say no. They never say maybe. They never say, "You were lousy."

Fantasies are rejection-proof. And the ones just ahead go beyond merely sparing the men from the need to ask for sex—at the risk of being refused—to actually allowing the woman to assume that power and responsibility.

The women are confident about sex here, just as they were in the previous chapter, but now it's their show.

Two for the Road

"David" is twenty-eight years old. He's a personnel administrator from Lyme, Connecticut, and has been married for two years.

My wife and I and three other couples were spending a weekend in New York City. It was late on a Saturday night, we were on our way back from the club and totally in the mood after some pretty dirty dancing. There wasn't room for all of us in one cab so Jill and I walked a block until we saw one headed our way with its light on. The fingers of my right hand were intertwined with those of her left, and it must have looked like we were celebrating a ninth-round knockout as we hailed the taxi.

As soon as I told the driver to take us to the hotel, Jill gave me a warm, moist, lingering kiss. Bingo! We started to fool around. My hand was under her skirt, and she was rubbing the bulge that had formed in my pants. She said, "I need you right now, I can't wait." The next thing I know, she pulls my penis out and jumps on top of me. She rips out the crotch area of her pantyhose, and I slide right in. She takes my hands and puts them under her blouse and on her nipples. I begin to pinch them and she says, "Harder." She is completely out of her gourd, moaning and groaning, and the cabby is watching from his rearview mirror in amazement. We pull up to a stoplight and everyone on the sidewalk is gaping at us.

My wife pushes my hand down so that I have two fingers on one side of my penis and three fingers on the other, so that every time she moves back and forth she is getting sensation from my hands and my penis. She finally comes as we pull up the hotel, but I haven't yet. I'm about to pull out but she won't let me because I'm still carrying a full load. Jill persists, right in front of the hotel, and rocks me until I let go. What a woman!

We asked David and some of the other men who helped us with research to talk a little more about their real sex lives, as opposed to the fantasies. I wanted to hear about their most memorable erotic moments. You'll see that in many cases plain old reality is far from dull. Also, there are common themes that overlap fantasy and reality.

I have a wonderful sex life and a very willing wife. We've done a lot of crazy things like mutual masturbation while driving; sex in our car in broad daylight in the parking lot of the local mall; sex while I was driving . . . she's on my lap facing me, and I drove looking over her shoulder. When our hormones hit, we can't control ourselves. We even had sex in a see-through glass elevator in Atlantic City. The best part of sex . . . cunnilingus.

Satisfying The Customer

"Eric" is forty-two and from Chicago. He owns a jewelry store in Manhattan. He describes himself as single and searching.

This woman enters my jewelry store. She has high heels on and a short, loose dress. She's not wearing any stockings, and her chest is nicely contoured in her dress but it is not busting out. She has long blonde hair and is the rich type . . . very well-kept sexy, about thirty years old, and definitely not uptight. The kind of rich girl that wants to get laid . . . no inhibitions whatsoever.

She's very aggressive, very flirtatious and begins to initiate the sexual scenario. It's obvious what she wants. "May I use a rest room?" she asks. "I'll lead the way, it's downstairs," I tell her, and I'm playing along, knowing that she has no intention of using it anyway. When we get down stairs, she says, "I just wanted to get you down here." She backs me up against a table, pins my hands down, and start kissing me. She steps back from the table and starts to strip, but won't let me touch her.

She takes off each item of clothing one by one, and when she's done there are only two things remaining . . . her high heels and her underwear. Then she starts to undress me, till the point that I'm absolutely naked. I turn her around and slide down her panties, and then I bend her over the table and put my penis in from the rear. I like having my balls slap her in the rear and seeing the ripples of her ass.

She begins to moan . . . and every time she moans a little louder, I drive it in even more. I won't let myself come. My control is excellent. I pull out and put her on the table, legs dangling over one side. I go down on her and my face is feeling her wetness. She tastes so sweet that I could do it all day. She holds my head down there and I stay obediently until her juices start pouring out. Then I slide her down a bit and pull her legs up to rest against my shoulders, standing, I put myself inside her.

We develop a rhythm that takes over. It sweeps us along. I come hard and heavy.

"Eric's" favorite real-life sex episode differs from the fantasy in that he is willing to risk rejection.

We were a bunch of guys down in Florida for a week's vacation. One night we went to this club. I can't remember the name but it was packed with girls, and they were all scantily dressed. So we're hanging out, here and there, and we got a bit bored and decided to go up and hang out by the balcony. We're looking down on the dance floor and I spot this good-looking girl. Long brown hair, lovely breasts and legs.

I went back downstairs to go after her. She was a bit older than me at the time; a really nice body. After hanging out at the club for a while, she came back to my hotel room. We started to fool around and my hormones were in an extremely high level of excitement. I'd been completely surrounded all night at the club with slews of gorgeous girls, whom I felt I couldn't approach, so my hard-on had been yearning to be set loose. And this girl gave my need immediate attention.

She went down on me and, let me tell you . . . the best blow job I've ever gotten in my whole life. She used her mouth and hands very well together . . . in and out . . . up and down . . . rhythmic, sensual and very arousing. My hard-on grew in her mouth, until I exploded. And when I came, I came in her hair, on the wall, on the floor. It was shooting out of me. Then, still semihard, I came on top of her, heated and strong, penetrating her and sucking her breasts.

We were like animals in heat . . . rocking, thrusting, sucking; no kissing, no cuddling—just emotionless sex, sex for sex's sake.

I pulled myself out and went down on her . . . I knew it felt good because she arched her back like a rainbow. With my tongue I teased her and probed the walls of her wet cunt until I felt her body shaking and trembling. I stopped and she let out a big sigh.

Electric Storm

"Lee," a twenty-seven-year-old operations assistant living in Montreal, Canada, starts off: "I've been in a relationship for approximately two years."

It's a rainy night . . . with lots of thunder and lightning. My girlfriend and I are under the covers of my bed, naked. She begins by massaging my body from behind, caressing my *derriere* and kissing the area behind my neck. As she slides her hands up and down my body, I can feel her breath following her hands. I flip on my back and she begins to massage my penis and testicles, gently stroking the area behind the testicles as well.

She takes her tongue and starts to lick my penis up and down its length. After licking and soft kisses, she takes my penis in her mouth and begins to move up and down . . . taking me out of her and putting me back in. After I come in her mouth, I go down on her and jab my tongue into her wetness. She tastes so fine and my penis is getting hard again for her.

I tease her clitoris with my tongue and my hard-on is increasing by the moment. I pull up onto her and put my penis inside. I rest my hands on either side of her face as though I was doing pushups on her, sliding my penis in and out. She feels so good. The sensation is pure pleasure as I slide in and out easily.

After penetrating this way for a while, I roll over with her on the bed so that she can be on top. I watch her breasts bouncing up and down as she moves back and forth . . . riding me. I can lift my head up so that her breasts can smack me every time she moves. I sit up and she wraps her arms around me and I put my head in her cleavage. Our bodies are riding one another, following each other's rhythms and needs.

We are absorbed in pleasing one another, and each thrust is heightened by the lightning that is striking at that moment. It's electrifying our bodies and creating this sexual energy that is making us devour each other.

We are kissing one another and sucking and licking each other's faces as we rock back and forth.

I pick her up and turn her round and shove her head underneath the pillow as I put myself in from behind.

Every time I penetrate her the top of her head bashes

against the headboard and I get more and more aroused. I put myself in as far as her anatomy will let me; the lightning is striking with such force I feel that I need to hide from it. Her body is my haven and I am invading it, burrowing into it and controlling it. She has crouched in a squat position with her legs wide open, and her breasts resting on her knees, pushed up against the headboard. I put my hand on her ass and I'm pushing her toward the headboard as I force myself inside her from behind. As a wave of heat overcomes me, and thunder strikes down from the heavens, my body shakes and trembles in orgasm.

"Lee's" take on his hottest sex experience is even more in keeping with the theme of women who initiate and control the sexual encounter:

It was an ordinary evening . . . my girlfriend and I were heading back to her place after dinner. As we walked in the door, she threw me against the door and started to tear my clothes off. She took her hand and stuck it down my pants and grabbed my penis and began to stroke it. She pushed me down onto the floor and told me to stay there. She moved about a foot away and started to take off her clothes in an extremely seductive manner. She undid her shirt and then slid her skirt off. She was wearing a tight bra that she was busting out of, as well as a garter belt that held up her stockings. She undid the clips and released the garters from her stockings, and slowly slid them off.

She pulled down her underwear and I noticed that she had shaved off her pubic hair . . . she looked so sexy. She came on top of me and took my penis and sat right down onto me. Her high heels, which she left on, dug into the side of my thighs.

She held my head in both hands and put it on her chest. I

began to suck her breasts and took her nipples in my fingers . . . twisting them lightly. She got up and pulled me by
my legs so that my back would be straight on the floor. She
sat down on my face and extended her body till she could
put my penis in her mouth. We licked and ate in the "69"
position, and I loved the new buff her, the shaved pussy. My
tongue penetrated deep inside and she took me all the way
into her mouth. Just as she sensed I was about to come, she
hit climax herself and its flow soaked my face; quickly, she
took me out of her mouth and pushed me onto my side.

She moved in front of me so that we would lie side by side
and I nuzzled my face in her neck and put myself in from
the rear. I wrapped my arm around her waist and pulled her
real close. Together like this, side by side, her legs were close
together, so it was difficult for me to penetrate . . . but that's
the way I like it. I put my arm around her and started to fondle her breasts and she pushed her body even closer to mine.
As my body began shaking, she pulled away from me and
put her hand on my penis and jerked me off until I reached
orgasm and came all over the place.

At The Water's Edge

"Vincent" is twenty-one years old. He's a a production assistant for a
major TV network. Has been seeing someone for seven or eight
months. "I'm monogamous." he says, "but she still has sexual relations
with other people. It bothers me but I don't want to let her go."

I picture the girl I am seeing in my fantasy. I'll refer to her
as "C." I picture the two of us on the beach. I adore public
displays of affection, even though this beach is entirely secluded. We are all alone. She is wearing a piece of lingerie, a

frilly teddy that is completely see-through. I can see her perfectly round nipples piercing through the lace.

Completely in touch with her own sexuality, she lies down on the towel and puts her knees up to take to the heavens. I just watch her. She takes her hand and puts it inside her until her back is in a perfect arch. She closes her eyes and enjoys the feeling of her own wetness. I lift the bottom of her teddy and follow the scent of her. When I reach her, I take her hand out and put my tongue in.

She begins rubbing her breasts and jerking up and down as I'm smacking and devouring her sex. I reach up her body until my hand is in between her breasts and I tear open her teddy from chest to legs in one motion. I move up and put my hardness between her breasts while she holds them together. I'm getting so aroused. I power myself onto her and she is taking me in and out of her mouth. I need her now.

I move down and put myself inside of her. She scrapes the length of my back with her nails as I'm driving it in. I'm invading her body in more ways than one . . . my penis is drilling her, my tongue is in her throat, and my hands are pinching her nipples with great force. The final thrust sends semen rushing throughout her body, seeming as if we had just become one.

Parisian Interlude

Once again, his favorite hot sex experience fits the theme, too.

I was visiting my girlfriend in France. She was going to spend the semester abroad, so I decided to pack it up and go for spring break. We were walking back from the movie theater, both well aware that something sexual was going to happen. Everything was right . . . the romantic city, the pouring rain that had made us sopping wet. No umbrellas, we wallowed in what the heavens were offering us.

We started to kiss in the streets, rubbing against one another's wet bodies . . . knowing what this was all leading to. When we finally got back to her apartment she started to take off my wet clothes. She rolled off my shirt over my head . . . she forcefully pulled down my pants, which were generously clinging to my thighs. And then she took her clothes off slowly and seductively, keeping eye contact with me at all times.

It was clear that she wanted to be in control. I loved every moment of her control. We lay on the bed and she directed my hand to her clitoris. I started probing it, stimulating her, wanting her to reach the very brink of her orgasm. While I stimulated her, she began to jerk me off, up and down with quick and hard motions. Both at the brink of our orgasms, she sat down on my face and put her face on my penis.

We began to taste each other, feel each other in our mouths. She circled the tip of my penis with her tongue and held the base of my penis straight up so that its entirety would enter her mouth. After our bodies were pulsating, and waves began to take over, she got up and spread her legs far apart for my penetration.

I entered her like a bulldozer and wrapped my arms around her waist. This time I was in control and she wasn't going anywhere. My penis was throbbing and I was dying to release all the energy that she had built up. I pulled her closer and closer, slapping my body against her as she moaned and groaned, and her body sucked up all my juices. Her legs were far apart for my penetration.

Union(s) Pacific

Back to the beach. "Tomás" is in his mid-forties. He is a real-estate agent in Santa Barbara, California. And having spent time in that area covering former president Ronald Reagan's summer vacations, I'll bet I even know the beach he's thinking about.

I'm sunbathing alone on a deserted California beach. I'm drowsing, half-asleep. My eyes are closed but I hear the sound of an approaching four-wheel-drive vehicle. Since I have my bathing suit on, it's no big deal and I just continue to lie there.

I hear a door slam, and another. There are no voices. Suddenly, about twenty seconds later, a hand is yanking down on the elastic waistband of my suit. I open my eyes and instinctively kick but my legs are being held down by two beautiful women with long blonde hair. A third has pinned my hands over my head and a fourth is working my suit down over my hips.

Strangely, they never speak, nor do I. In an instant I'm naked and spread-eagled on the beach. The girl who stripped off the suit, a redhead with a gorgeous body and wearing a string bikini, starts gobbling my dick, which gets hard in a flash. She strokes it with her right hand and sucks deeply.

The women take turns blowing me. They stop and switch off just before I'm about to come. The blondes holding my legs spread them apart and the redhead stands between them and slowly removes the top and bottom of her bikini. She smiles, straddles me and settles down on my flagpole, rocking back and forth.

She starts slowly and builds momentum, faster and faster. Her eyes roll back into her head. She smiles a Mona Lisa smile. The ride seems to last for hours. I come explosively but to my amazement don't lose my erection. In turn, each of the other women mount me. Sweating and bucking, I blast each of them with scorching streams of semen.

After the last women has been satisfied, without a word the four of them put their bikinis back on, climb into their shiny Range Rover and depart. I'm too exhausted to even think about writing down their license plate number.

In the years that I've spent on my unique beat as a reporter covering the relationships between men and women, I have learned that men see themselves as having two primary functions: effective, desirable lovers and competent breadwinners. This is probably both a cultural and a biological imperative. It is tangled up with the survival and evolution of the species. The strongest and smartest hunter mated with women who knew their young would be fed and protected sufficiently to grow up. His genetic characteristics were transferred, the children lived to maturity, began the mating cycle all over again and so on from the cave to the condo.

Today, though, condo woman doesn't need cave man's muscle power or aggressiveness to guarantee the well-being of her offspring. That one vital male role is therefore diminished. I think this creates more pressure on the remaining effective-lover role. There's only so much inner strength to be derived from watching Monday night football, polishing off a six-pack or filling a sales quota. The result is a hunger for sexual satisfaction combined with a buildup of stress and anxiety that makes the possibility of rejection so threatening and painful.

Am I telling you that men exist solely to screw and work? Don't press me. I might have to say yes. A qualified yes. There are other roles, important ones, but none outweigh the roles of lover and breadwinner. Men want to succeed in this lover role to the point that they are willing to at least fantasize about giving up sexual power and control. They are getting off on imaginary sexual encounters that do not involve being in charge of when and where and how the sex takes place.

They like those fantasies. They get to be effective and desirable lovers because the women they love have been liberated from the tyranny of sexual subservience.

That's very good news, indeed.

Three

Secrets
of Innocence:
Older Women

A friend of mine married a much younger woman, another dates a woman who's only a few years older than his daughter. Recently, on a street in Brooklyn I noticed two guys in their sixties interrupt their chat to admire a gorgeous twenty-something African-American woman stroll by. Scientists and researchers call this anecdotal evidence, and before I started this book I could have been convinced, by these examples and many others, that a favorite male fantasy is one that involves older men and younger women.

Now I know better.

In the fantasy department, it is just the reverse: older women and younger men.

Before you start citing incidents of menopausal males running off with bimbos a third their age, let me add this salient point: I'm talking fantasy here, not reality.

And in reality, the mythic "girl from Ipanema," is lusted after by men and boys of all ages. They eyeball, they flirt, they hit on and make it (or want to make it) with sexy women who are years younger than themselves. Attempting to cure a midlife crisis by "robbing the cradle" is an ancient, if not honorable, practice.

Yes, men like younger women. Strangely enough, though, they don't seem to fantasize about it all that much. Not in terms of fully developed scripts and scenarios that they play back to themselves again and again.

There may be something to be said for minifantasies versus maxifantasies. In this case, a minifantasy would be the flash of lust: "Wow, she's cute. I'd love to . . ." A maxifantasy is more elaborate and often involves a structure that is similar to a story with a beginning, a middle and an end.

A minifantasy is akin to a mosquito bite. It itches and you scratch it. The sensation is immediate and so is the gratification. The maxifantasy aches and emanates from deep beneath the skin. It lingers.

I think this distinction helps explain the seeming contradiction. Another important aspect of it is that when men fantasize they are *idealizing*. What happens in the fantasy is the embodiment—"inheadment"?—of perfection. The guy imagines himself at an ideal age. He may actually be seventy years old but sees himself as either a much younger man or as an ageless man. Sexual fantasies are the fountain of youth. A man remains a desirable, effective lover in his own fantasies no matter what his age or circumstances. And that is the reason, as far as I'm concerned, for having a fantasy in the first place.

Hence, it's not surprising that older man and younger woman fantasies aren't more common. Their partners may be young but the men don't usually see themselves as old. Even in fantasies where the woman is cast as inexperienced and innocent, the men tend to have sexual know-how without wrinkles and gray hair.

Casting the guy as the inexperienced innocent, on the other hand, is what makes the older woman and younger man fantasy so appealing.

It allows men to relive those "thrilling days of yesteryear," when they were, in fact, relatively innocent and inexperienced. It was a time when the male aspiration to be a desirable and effective lover had a natural counterweight that served to relieve some of the pressure and anxiety. To put it simply: "I'm only sixteen years old. Of course I'm going to come in .003 seconds."

The older-woman fantasy is another version of no-fault sex. Control and responsibility are shifted to the woman. She obviously desires this sixteen-, eighteen- or twenty-year-old guy. It's purely sexual. As a rule, a thirty-year-old woman does not get off on an eighteen-year-old's mind and range of experiences. She wants his body. Period.

And that's what a lot of guys want to be wanted for. With the older-woman fantasy there is no danger of rejection, no performance anxiety, no commitments.

Like the confident woman and the woman who initiates, the older woman has control, but she is not assuming it from him or sharing it. Control is hers by right. He is the passive partner, not through any act or inclination of his own, but as a result of forces beyond his control—her age and his lack of experience.

In this fantasy, men do not need to relinquish control. They don't have it to begin with. As a result, from the standpoint of confronting inner conflicts, there's no need to deal with the desire to assume an "unnatural" male sexual role. What happens, happens. The benefits are there without having to risk consciously entertaining seditious notions about sexual equality or whether she might like to occasionally take charge of the whole glorious erotic production from the casting call to the final cut.

For adults, pleasure always has a price. Sexual pleasure is no different. This fantasy theme is an attempt to repeal that fact of life. It is saying there can be sex without even the need to satisfy your partner, a need that is a fundamental part of male identity. Giving up that role distills sex to its pure physical essence. There's no other baggage aside from

pleasure. That may be a concept that's hard to accept for many people—men and women—but it is one that is at the heart of the older
woman and younger man fantasy and the desires it reflects.

We are conditioned to load sex with a heavy burden: love, intimacy,
commitment, sharing, procreation. This recurring fantasy theme seeks
to drastically lighten up the sexual dynamic. I find it very appealing
and very subversive. Sex encumbered like a pack mule will never be
more than a beast of burden. It won't trot, or gallop—or soar on the
wings of Pegasus. I applaud any attempt, fantasy or otherwise, to just
let sex be sex.

As for subversion, this fantasy is another step toward a great power
shift. Through it, the message is being sent that men can find pleasure
and satisfaction in sex refined to its most basic level. Not power, not
dominance, not ego—pleasure.

I think if women are looking for signs of a new sexual age, an erotic
enlightenment that promises to be a damned sight better than the status quo, there are glimmers of it in the fantasies ahead in this chapter.

The Perfect Martini

"Alberto" is a thirty-three-year-old chef, living in Tempe, Arizona. He
and his girlfriend have been together five years.

> One of my sexual fantasies involves an older woman. She is
> not someone I know, but in my fantasy she is extremely real.
> Older women, in my mind, are more mature, more in con-
> trol. Anyway, my fantasy goes like this: I'm at a bar and no-
> tice this attractive older woman sitting on a stool, about ten
> seats away from me. I would say she is about fifty years old
> and has the laugh-lines to prove it, but is extremely sexy.
> Her wavy brown hair is halfway down her back, and she is

wearing a black top that is hugging her tits. That's about all I can see from where I'm sitting.

She takes out a gold case from her bag, which is holding her cigarettes. She lights one, looks at me and gives me a wink. This is my cue . . . I walk over and offer to buy her a drink . . . she accepts, "A Martini, with three olives, please." She takes an olive on the toothpick and starts to lick the alcohol off it. Her tongue is circling it, licking it, but she won't put it in. This phallic display is making me crazy. I ask her, "Is this how you treat your men as well?" She laughs. Before I know it, she is fondling my fly. I look down and notice that the black top is the only article of clothing that she is wearing. She takes her legs and uncrosses them on the bar stool facing me. I see everything.

I take my finger and put it inside of her. "No," she says, "I'm in control!" She pulls my penis out of my pants and comes and sits on top of me. People are watching, and the more they watch, the wilder she gets . . . she is riding me ferociously, driving her tongue down my throat. She takes my head and puts it between her creamy breasts, holding it there.

I take my hands and I grab her ass and really push her into me. The bar stool is shaking and everyone has their eyes on us. After a few final thrusts, we come simultaneously; she gets up, lights a cigarette and moves to the other end of the bar. No holding, no cuddling, just pure pleasure.

A Green . . . Thumb?

This next fantasy is from "Art," a forty-eight-year-old travel agent from Eugene, Oregon. He's married with four children.

I'm probably seventeen in the fantasy and still a virgin although I masturbate a lot. My parents are away for the weekend. Mom's best friend has just moved into a new house and she asked me to go over and help her get the overgrown garden under control. It's hot, I'm working in my cutoff shorts without a shirt. Very sweaty. Mrs. Philips is probably in her mid-forties, slim but not what you would call sexy. She's on the prim side. Her husband is on a business trip.

I can tell she's looking at me as I bend over to weed. At one point she passes by and wipes the sweat off my back with the palm of her hand and laughs. Mrs. Philips makes sandwiches for lunch. We eat on her patio, making small talk. She asks about high school and my girlfriend, whose name is Donna. She teases me about Donna and asks if we drive down to the river to park and watch the submarine races. It's embarrassing.

After lunch, there's more work in the garden and I notice that Mrs. Philips is wearing tight jeans and a pair of low-heeled cowboy boots. for a second I imagine Donna naked in those boots. At the end of the day, Mrs. Philips invites me in for a beer. She disappears and I hear the shower running. She comes back and tells me that I should clean up before I go home. I try to beg off but she insists and leads me to her bedroom. She says I can undress in there and toss my clothes out into the hall so that she can quickly wash and dry them. I do as I'm told but it makes me feel strange.

I wrap a towel around my waist and duck into the bathroom. I'm in the shower soaping up when I hear the door open. A second later, Mrs. Philips slips into the shower with me. She's only wearing those boots. She moves behind me and begins washing my back. My prick feels like it is about to explode. Mrs. Philips asks me if I've ever screwed Donna.

I can hardly stammer out an answer. I tell her no, not yet. She says good and promises to show me how. She reaches around and starts stroking my prick.

Of course I come almost immediately. We finish in the shower and Mrs. Philips takes me by the hand into her bedroom, pushes me down on the bed and kisses my balls until I'm up again. She straddles me and inserts my prick into her and starts to glide up and down.

I stay the night and all the next day. I'm now forty-eight and have had this fantasy for more than twenty years. It's a wonderful turn-on.

Who's in charge here? He certainly isn't. "Art's" fantasy is not only about losing one's virginity and having a weekend of great sex, it's also about giving up control to a woman who enjoys sex and knows what she's doing. The fact that this particular fantasy has had a shelf-life of over twenty years suggests its power. The boy has grown up but hasn't outgrown the image of the experienced, sexually aggressive woman. Here's to you, Mrs. Philips.

Child Care

Here's another quickie fantasy along the same lines from a different man, "Ben," thirty-nine, the manager of a dry-cleaning operation in Williamsport, Pennsylvania. It mixes fact and fiction:

I've fantasized about older partners, and two come to mind—a baby-sitter and a guidance counselor I had in high school. The baby-sitter allowed me to massage her legs and sit between her legs and look up her dress. I was too inexperienced at the time to take it any further.

The guidance counselor was at least in her late forties, I

was about seventeen. Nothing actually happened except in my mind, but I was attracted to her and wanted her to take the initiative and "counsel" me in the mysteries of sex.

I also have fantasies of any situation where the woman takes charge of the activity.

Special Delivery

"Tyler" is twenty-seven years old. He lives in New Rochelle, New York, and works in the garment industry, marking and grading women's clothing. He told us that he'd just become engaged to the woman he had been dating for four and a half years. "Tyler" proposed on the scoreboard at halftime during a New York Knicks game. "Thank God she accepted," "Tyler" said.

I'm in my early twenties and I'm a food delivery man . . . which at the time I was actually doing. Anyway, I'm on my route. I pull up to this apartment building and buzz the woman's name.

The intercom crackles and she tells me to push penthouse and come right up. I get up there, ring the bell, and she opens the door dressed in a silk robe. I'd say she was about forty-five years old but still very slim and sexy.

"Please come inside for a moment while I get some money," she tells me. I enter the apartment and close the door behind me. She goes into her bedroom and says, "Could you please bring the food in here?" I follow the sound of her voice and walk into the bedroom. She has taken her robe off and is pulling the satin sheets between her legs, looking at me with corrupting eyes. I don't know where to look first—her jugs, her pussy or what.

"If you want your money, you'll have to come and get it,"

she says. I approach the bed and she puts her twenty-dollar bill between the lips of her vagina. "If you want your money, you'll have to come and get it," she repeats. My hand lowers to grab the twenty, but she shakes her head. "No, with your mouth."

She takes my hand and pulls me down to the bed. She pushes my body around so that she is over me and my face is in her wetness. I stick my tongue in her vagina and curl it around the twenty-dollar bill. I take the money and throw it on the nightstand. She keeps my head in place with her hands.

I probe her clit with my tongue and start to taste her. She pulls me up and kisses me. She unzips my fly, reaches in and pulls out my bulging hard-on. She pushes me on top of her, opens her legs real wide, and plunges me into her hot and wet slit. She looks me in the eyes and says, "Fuck me hard." I throw my arms around her and grab her ass as I violate her body with my rod.

I push my face between her size D breasts. I hold her ass real tight and flip her on the bed so that she is on top of me. I tell her, "Now you fuck me hard." She grabs the crossbar between the bed posts and starts to ride me like a horse. I lift my face so that her breasts will smack me in the face and so that I can suck them every now and then. She is moaning like a madwoman, and I grab her hips to increase the pace of her grinding. I start to lift her up and down onto my hard-on feeling the lips of her vagina smack against my body like a suction cup.

I take her legs and spread them to each side of the bed, so that I can penetrate deeper and deeper.

I take her breasts into my hands and jerk her body on mine, pulling her like a jockey on my penis. Our bodies be-gin to shake from arousal and our bodies pour into one another. She lowers herself onto my body and licks my penis clean. She rests her head on my thighs and wraps her arm tenderly around my waist.

Summer in the Suburbs

"Kevin" is thirty years old and works in a copy shop in Green Bay, Wisconsin, but says this fantasy is set in Sacramento, California, where he grew up.

It was the second summer that I had been doing yard work for the Franklins on Thursday afternoons, so I knew all the rules—how Mr. Franklin expected the lawn to be seamless and edged just so; how the hedges had to be trimmed and the bed underneath raked of all debris; how to clean the swimming pool to perfection—before rinsing off the clippings and sweat in the outdoor shower and jumping in. And how, if my check wasn't underneath the mat outside the back door, I was to knock for Mrs. Franklin—Carole— since Mr. Franklin was out "golfing" all day Thursday. It was hard work for a kid just getting into high school, but hey, twenty bucks used to mean something.

I had only been in the house twice—once when I was hired, and one time when Mr. Franklin had forgotten to write my check before leaving. What was striking about the inside of the house was that one whole wall of the living room was mirrored. And that's how it all got started.

That day I had finished the lawn and trimmed the shrubs. The front beds were done, and I was just starting the beds in the back under the windows of the living room. I had to crawl on hands and knees between the shrubs and the house and rake the ground clean and smooth as I backed out. Hot and cramped, I paused and lifted my head to stretch. That's when I saw Carole.

Or rather, I saw her reflection in the mirrored wall of the living room. It was the motion that caught my eye—she was in her bedroom exercising, but most of all she was completely naked.

I knelt, transfixed, not daring to move, as I watched her twist and flail, spin and kick. She couldn't have been much more than thirty, and her exercises were having the desired effect—she was fit and trim, from her slim, firm calves, to her slender hips, past her flat, featureless stomach, to her upswept breasts, over shoulders and arms with just a hint of muscle and sinew, to cheeks flushed with effort. Her raven-black hair, trimmed short as was the style then, was pasted to her forehead and nape in sweat-slicked spearpoints.

It was clear that she took every advantage of the poolside. Every inch of Carole's body glowed with a caramel tan—except for two ivory triangles around her rosebud nipples and a narrow white frame just outside the short, tousled blackness between her hips.

It was only as she walked into view that I realized the pounding, rushing sound in my head, the fiery burn of my face and the edges of my ears—the ache of my neck from craning to see. I looked about, sure that my crime had been noted—of course not, I was in the backyard, behind a fence! I scurried out and for once showered before I cleaned the pool—blessed cool relief.

Still, I fretted, all week, knowing that at any moment I would be called to account for my sins—but the call never came.

The next Thursday I tried with all my might to do nothing different, sure that in spite of my efforts at normalcy I would be found out—but that did not stop me from seeking, as before, the sight that had so torn my sleep the past seven nights.

My wait was not in vain. Once again, and for weeks thereafter, I became intimate with every detail of Carole's form—followed by that shower!

It came to an end, so to speak, one Thursday as I dallied at the side of the house, preparing to mow the lawn. Mr. Franklin's convertible was still out front—he was usually gone by the time I got there. I heard voices from within the house, voices first angry, then angrier. The front door banged open, exploding the argument of Carole and her husband onto the porch. He heaved his golf clubs into the back of the car, chased by Carole, who was loosely wrapped by a white terry robe.

"Go on, you bastard, go see her," Carole was shouting. "Get your ass out of here!"

"Go get fucked . . . if you can, you bitch—if you haven't forgotten how!" he yelled back.

He got into the car as epithets flew and roared off, tires screaming. The front door slammed—and all was quiet. I waited a few minutes, then began my chores, not knowing what else to do.

The morning passed otherwise uneventfully, even to the point of Carole's regular exercise routine, which by now I knew by heart. But this time, in the middle of her kicking exercises, she faltered, then collapsed to the floor, her head buried in her hands, sobbing. I felt so helpless and empty for her—so sad, in fact, that I almost didn't react when she lifted her tear-streaked face and gazed—right into my eyes!

I wrenched my face away, hoping she hadn't seen, knowing she had. Keeping my head down, I finished the bed, then hurried to the shower and cleaned the pool, not once hazarding a peek at the house. I collected my check and left.

Thursday came again, and all seemed normal. There was no car out front, no argument—but this time I avoided the rear bed entirely, never once risking a look into that window. I finished the pool and lifted the mat—no check. Damn.

My knock at the back door was answered in only a moment. Carole stood in the doorway, her terry-cloth robe exposing a deep V over her rhythmically pulsing chest, her hair matted with sweat as I had seen it so often before.

My discomfort was becoming more and more apparent. I asked for my check. "You haven't finished the back beds," she said, and closed the door.

I retrieved the rake and crawled behind the bushes, swearing I wouldn't look up—but I had to. I raised my eyes—and met Carole's. She was standing, robed, in her bedroom. Slowly, our eyes locked, she loosened the robe and let it slide off her shoulders onto the floor around her ankles. The words she mouthed were unmistakable—"Come here."

Everything seemed so far away as I turned the doorknob and followed the cool tile hallway into her bedroom. I stopped ten feet away from her, a statue. She moved across the room until she was only inches from me, and a scent unlike any I had known before wafted over me. It was perfume and sweat and . . . woman. Her fingers grasped my hand and lifted it, placing it upon her left breast, my fingers touching her erect, hard nipple. Slowly, ever so slowly, she drew my hand down, down, so my fingertips gently caressed her skin. Then she lifted my other hand to do the same thing to her other breast. Time and time again, she repeated the motion, first one hand then the other, closing her eyes and lifting her chin, then rolling her head to one side, now quietly ohing and ahing.

At last, bringing her eyes to mine and placing my hands on her shoulders, and hers on my waist, she backed to the bed and sat upon it. He fingers deftly loosened my cutoff jeans, then slid them expertly to my ankles. She lifted my briefs over my erect, pulsing organ, dispatching them as well, and stood once more. Placing her hands now on either side of my face, she pulled our mouths together, her tongue parting my lips as she formed her body to mine. The softness of her breasts against my smooth, boyish chest, the tickle of her pubic furriness, the scents, the tastes—she moved just so, sliding her firm belly against my hardness— and I came.

Weak-kneed, I staggered to the bed to sit, then lie back upon it. She was smiling with kindness and caring, her tanned body glistening with the syrup of my ejaculation. I tried to apologize, but she shushed me, and lay beside me, touching my now-spent member. She bent down, taking it into her mouth, rolling it with her tongue, licking. Such pleasure I had never known before—but I would know better.

In no time, I was hard and stiff again, courtesy of her skillful mouth. Rolling onto her back, she spread her legs apart and drew my hands down to touch her wet creamy opening. "Touch me here," she said, "Now—gently!— rub . . . yes, that way . . . slowly . . . yes . . . now, touch my nipples . . . easy! Don't hurry." Taking my hand in hers once more, she showed me her pleasure—until, with eyes closed, breath coming in pants, she gasped, "Now, come in me."

Carole lifted her knees wide and I rolled between her legs. She pulled me to her, rocking and bucking, then wrapped her legs and arms around my back. I reached around to direct myself into her—and felt for the first time that ecstasy of a man as I slipped inside, coming in only moments. She came shortly thereafter, and at first I thought I had hurt her. But the quivering breaths and the half-smile on her lips told me otherwise.

We lay there for what seemed like hours, the warmth and wetness of our passion cooling into the coldness of reality. I could feel myself shrinking, slipping out of her, the fluids we had shared drying. At long last we separated, and I felt ashamed. Carole sensed that and pulled me to her once more. "Never be ashamed of giving pleasure to a woman," was all she said.

We dressed, me in my cutoffs, she in her bikini, and swam together, laughing. That wasn't the last time we made love—she taught me a lot in the time we had together—but before the end of the summer, she was divorced and had moved away.

I miss her sometimes.

Was this all fantasy—or were parts real? Or did it happen just as I tell myself it did? Who's to say.

A Society Ball

"Roy" is twenty-five. Married for just over a year, he's an appliance repairman from Nashville, Tennessee. He offered us a fantasy that he says he enjoys on an average of once a week.

I visualize myself at a dance where the women are good-looking. They don't have to be young, though. Many women in their forties and fifties (possibly even sixties) are extremely well-preserved—especially those who are married to wealthy men who choose the prettiest ones for their wives and then pamper them with the good life so they can keep their figures and gorgeous complexions. An example of a dance with this type of women would be a society ball.

Anyway, my fantasy is that at a certain instant everyone in the room is frozen in place and has no knowledge of what's going on around them. The men are all off in one corner away from the action. (Incidentally, at the end of all this no one remembers what has gone on—except me. Time has not passed, watches and clocks remain as they were.)

The women take their clothes off as I approach them, and sometime I imagine that this disrobing takes place en mass. I then have the opportunity to caress the breasts, the vulva, vaginal lips, clitoris, vagina and entire body of every woman in the room.

As I give them orgasms manually or by cunnilingus, they moan and their bodies jerk erotically. Some of them ejaculate a few squirts from their urethras (not urine). Some have tampons in their vaginas, which I pull out and then replace.

I inhale the aroma of all these beautiful pussies. The women are not stiff in their places, although "unconscious," but are extremely pliable in my hands.

Sometimes I insert my penis in every lady in the room to see how each one feels. I don't really fuck them because that would make me tired and unable to enjoy all the female bodies in the room. Usually I do fuck the last one or two. Then, at my signal, all the ladies get dressed again and their men rejoin them. No one—except me—being the wiser as to what has just happened.

I detect a lot of Peter Pan in "Roy" and the other men in this chapter. The fantasies relieve them of the need to grow up (in this imaginative context, that is). They can be forever boys with magical powers. "Roy" can stop time in the ballroom, satisfy his curiosity and desire, and then jump-start reality once again as if nothing had happened.

And isn't that the ideal sexual paradigm? Ideally, making love for a few minutes or a few hours stops the clock and banishes the real world from the bedroom. At its best, there is a magic that distinguishes sex from the other sensual pleasures. Perhaps it is the combination of all five senses acutely heightened in their intensity.

I also get the feeling that the older woman and younger man fantasy derives much of its attraction to men from the fact that it not likely to happen for real. There is a generational divide that tends to discourage traffic flow from the direction of older women toward younger men. It does happen, but not that frequently. This makes the fantasy more desirable because, one, it is unusual and somewhat of a taboo, and, two, it doesn't end up nagging a guy about whether he should try to live it out.

If there's a downside to fantasies in general, it is this nasty little habit they have of whispering, "Hey, let's give it a try. What are you, chicken?" I'm forever warning men to think twice about trying to fulfill fantasies. Just enjoy them as fantasies.

The theme of the young man being initiated by an attractive neighbor lady is almost quaint. A guy at twenty-five or fifty-five can still look back on the fantasy-possibility with great pleasure. It implies no moral judgment one way or another. He's not a pervert or a sicko, just a kid who got lucky.

I think women can read this fantasy as confirmation that behind many bluff, ironclad males facades lurks a hunger for sex that is closer to innocence that they might otherwise assume. Innocence in the sense of being without the scar tissue and calluses that build up over time to deaden the joy.

And then there's the universal theme of starting over. But that's the stuff of epic poetry and novels—and I promised you a book of fantasies.

Four

Secrets of Strangers: Anonymous Sex

The one-night stand. The ultimate smoking gun to prove that men are jerks.

Hold on a minute. Let's treat the fantasy notions of having great sex with anonymous women for what they really are: fantasies, products of the imagination, self-service fiction.

Without doubt, there's meaning and substance present that is worth digging for, but it may not amount to the sum total of meaning and substance commonly ascribed to the *act* of having sex with strangers.

The *act.*

And that is? I thought you'd ask, and my answer, while sounding politically correct, is correct from a practical standpoint: Sex with strangers—the one-night stand of reality—is selfish and promiscuous sex, exploitative and hurtful sex, and predatory sex. And lest I forget, dangerous sex.

This is all true. Probably. And true, probably, for both men and women. But fantasies, when they remain such, are *not* true. Yet, there is meaning, and it is different and deeper.

I see the theme as an attempt by men to nudge sex back toward a lost ideal. In the safe haven of the head and heart, men are freed from social conventions that are in conflict with who they are and what they desire.

This who and what combination isn't necessarily very exotic. Mostly, the theme of sex with a stranger is to sexuality what a convenience store is to food. You get in, get it and get out.

It is such a common and robust scenario that I think that the men who have these fantasies are not hitting the real-life sexual "7-Elevens" all that often, or at all. Otherwise, why fantasize? Just do it and save your imaginative energy for golden showers or cross-dressing.

Rather than confirming that men are jerks or sexual predators, these fantasies may be telling us just the opposite. They are satisfying a sexual desire, that is perhaps a natural one, through the outlet of fantasy, not reality. Instead of hustling for promiscuous sex, they are imagining it.

I tend to buy the theory that men are biologically or genetically programmed to have sex frequently with whatever mature women are available. It's a way to propagate the species fast and efficiently. But men are social creatures, too. Some conventions do have permanent affects. Several thousand years of pairing off for various social reasons—practicality, conflict avoidance, security, hygiene, whatever—aren't easily ignored. Modern men may want to screw whomever whenever, but they know deep down that it isn't a particularly good idea.

Enter the fantasy. It works for him without creating crippling social problems and potentially devastating internal conflicts. He can have one-night stands three times a day without being hurtful and selfish.

I seriously doubt that this fantasy theme would survive for long, both as fantasy or reality, if it were somehow put into actual practice on a routine basis. In the end, sex with strangers is an unnatural act. And I don't mean that solely in terms of social conventions. Sex is a powerful bonding mechanism that exerts a countervailing influence on the instinct to breed indiscriminately.

I've talked to psychologist after psychologist who believes that habitual promiscuous sex is a symptom of psychological disorder. Men and women who isolate themselves from others, who withdraw from physical and emotional intimacy, are not only violating a social convention, they are in conflict with a human need. This species of ours didn't survive and develop in isolation, one from another. Sex is an elemental connector, perhaps the most elemental. It joins man to woman and leads to the link between parents and children.

The sex-with-strangers fantasy is an ingenious way around all of this. Men can screw as much as they want with whomever they want and not screw themselves in the process.

It seems like a pretty good compromise to me. As you read the fantasies in this chapter it may help to view them in those terms.

Road Work

"Chris" is a thirty-one-year-old engineer living in Manhattan. He says, "I've been in a relationship for almost two years. We knew each other in college and I was always attracted to her but she never paid much attention to me. I bumped into her at a Pavarotti concert in Central Park and we've been dating since then.

This fantasy is actually half-fantasy and half-reality.

I used to have a house in the Hamptons and would go out there pretty much every weekend. One time on my way out, I saw a hitchhiker on the highway. She was a tall, lean black woman, standing on the side of the road with a knapsack hanging from her shoulders.

I pulled onto the side of the road and asked her "Where are you headed?" "I'm going to Montauk for the weekend," she said.

"Well, I'm going out halfway if you'd like a ride."

She shrugged her shoulders, opened the passenger door and climbed right in. She sat with her hands folded on her legs in her extremely short skirt. She was very attractive, and I just wanted to pull off to the side of the road and have my way with her.

This is where my fantasy takes over. So we are driving for a while, and she keeps fiddling with the radio and every time she changes the station, she makes a conscious effort to brush her arm against my leg. Her skin feels so soft against my leg and I can sense her eyes fixed on me as I drive. The traffic puts us at a standstill, so I look at her until our eyes meet. She is so beautiful that I want to feel myself inside her.

She leans over and kisses me on the cheek very innocently. I take my hand and run it up and down her thighs. She widens her legs and gives me the cue that she would like to be touched. I take my fingers and pry them between the crotch area of her shorts. She arches her back and tilts her head back into the seat.

"Would you like to pull over and wait for the traffic to die down a bit?" she asks me. I take my hand and run it over her breast and say, "I'd like that." I wheel the car into a rest area and park strategically behind a huge spruce tree.

The moment I turn the ignition off, she leaps on top of me and starts to intensely kiss me. She takes her tongue and jabs it down my throat with conviction. I take my hand and put it underneath her blouse. I hold her breasts and manipulate them in my hands. I can feel the warmth of her vagina radiating through her panties as she rubs against my leg.

I slide off her underwear and stick my fingers inside of her. She is so wet I want to slide myself inside of her, and she takes my penis out of my pants so that I can do just that. She lifts her hips up and sits right down on my bulging hard-on. She begins to rock back and forth with her ass jammed against the steering wheel. I place my face in between her luscious breasts and lick them and suck them every chance I get.

I lift her up and turn her around so that her body is slouched over the steering wheel. Holding her hips, I lower her ass onto my hard-on and slide her up and down. Her ass is smacking against me, and between the moans of her pleasure and the bouncing of flesh against one another, I am shoving myself deeper and deeper inside her. I take my hands and manually stimulate her clit while I drive myself in; I can feel it hardening between my finger tips.

We are fucking one another so hard that the car has turned into a steam pit and we can't see through the windows. I can hear her last gasps of breath before that brink of orgasmic pleasure. I speed up my thrusts and we both come pouring out all over the place.

"Chris's" real-life hot sex episode is strikingly similar thematically. The woman is also very much a stranger. This fact seems central to his pleasure.

I was in a bar on the West Side and met this flight attendant for Lufthansa.

She was a very striking woman with a big chest and ocean-blue eyes. I could tell she was getting ready to leave and followed her outside and watched her hail a cab. As she got into the cab, she turned around and gave me a look. Her eyes were calling me, so I ran over. "I have a room at the Hyatt for the evening, would you like to join me?"

"I would love to," I said as she moved over in the cab so that I could get in. The ride to the hotel was somewhat awkward because we both knew what kind of night it was going to be.

At the Hyatt, we sat in her room sipping wine and talk-ing dirty. "Are you circumcised?" she asked me. "Because most American men are." I nodded. "Tell me how big you are." "You'll have to find out for yourself," I answered, crossing my fingers in the hopes that she would touch me right then and there. The conversation was completely arousing me and the next thing I know, she gets up and goes into the bathroom. At this point, I didn't know if she was going to come out in the buff and if I should undress, or what the hell I should do. I decide on a 50 percent ballsy move and just take my shirt off as if I was hot or something.

When she finally emerges from the bathroom, to my de-light, she's completely naked. She lay down on the bed and motioned for me to come over. I got down next to her and let my fingers glide up and down her body. She took my hand and poked my fingers inside of her, moving them around her wetness. She got up into a squat position and started to lower herself up and down onto my hand so that her ass was smacking against my palm.

After humping my hand for a couple of minutes, her come came dribbling down my hand. She lay down and started to unzip my pants and take out my hard-on. She gripped my penis in both her hands and started to jerk me off. But I was in the mood for something more wet . . . I lifted her up and pulled her right down onto me so that she could ride me. My penis swam around in her juices and she began to rock me back and forth aggressively.

I took her hips in my hands to help make her thrusts faster and faster. She wrapped her arms around the bedpost and started to sit up and down on my hard-on but I needed to kiss her. We flipped on the bed so that we were in the mis-sionary position. I wrapped my arms around and put my hands on her ass so that I could control my penetration.

If I wanted to enter her real deep, then I would clench her ass and bring it toward me. I stabbed my tongue inside her mouth, and the different wetnesses were crazily arousing me. She pushed me off of her and put her back against the wall with one leg suspended in midair. I went over to her, holding her leg in that position over my arm and penetrating deep inside her. Every time I went in, her ass was banging against the wall and her pain was making me fuck her harder and harder.

I really needed to rip through before I came, so I took her by the hand and led her into the bathroom. I threw her body over the sink and drove myself in from the rear. I slung my hands around her and took her breasts into my hands and I continued to rip into her. I held her real tight as I inhaled deeply, and jerked in and out of her in quick motions . . . the last thing that I remember is that I saw stars that night!

When It Rains

"Jesse" is a headhunter living in Cleveland. He's twenty-five years old. "As far as relationships go," he says, "I don't really have a significant one . . . I guess I'd say I was single and dating."

I am walking on a secluded city street in the pouring rain . . . actually, it's a torrential downpour. There is no one around when I bump into this stunning foreign woman. She is wearing a short flimsy dress, which is clinging to her body from the rain, and we immediately find shelter in one another's flesh.

We have this passionate exchange with our eyes and then we start on some heavy-duty kissing. There is nothing to say . . . it's an understood attraction. I start to tear her clothes off and slide the tattered dress down over her wet body. I move my tongue up and down her body and we are pressed against one another. She throws me against the wall and sticks her hand inside my pants, fondling my penis. The rain is pounding on our bodies and we are in a fit of almost angry passion.

I pushed her up against the wall and stick my fingers inside of her. She is drinking the rain as it slaps her in the face and I am licking it off her breasts. I grab her size-two body, spread her legs apart, and hold her up against the wall. I pull out my bulging hard-on and put it inside of her. She wraps her arms around my neck and as I drive myself into her the brick makes impressions on her back.

I rest my head in between her breasts and lick the water that runs down her cleavage. She is incessantly repeating the same phrase—"Ay dios mio . . . Ay dios mio"—and the more she talks to me in Spanish, the more aroused I become and the harder I push my penis inside of her. I pull myself out and have her turn around, placing her hands palm down on the brick wall. It looks like I am arresting her and I frisk her body up and down, sticking my fingers inside her and rubbing my body against hers.

I push her legs apart and stick myself in from behind. I rest my hands on top of hers, facing the brick wall, and jam my body into hers with her wet vagina slapping against the wall. The rain at this point is ripping into our skins and we are moving to the rhythm of the heavy pitter-patter. I throw my arms around her and grab her breasts . . . protecting them from the harsh brick wall.

I start to move in and out of her in sharp, quick motions, not allowing my penis to escape the sanctuary of her warm wetness. As my body and hers begin to shake, I squeeze her breasts extremely hard, and we come simultaneously. The rain cleans our juices off our bodies, and we part like two strangers in the night.

The following may be the ultimate sex-with-a-stranger fantasy, but it involves "Jesse's" girlfriend and a real sexual experience. It's another example of how needs and desires that are expressed in fantasies blend into real life.

I was in college and it was in between semesters, summertime. My girlfriend and I lived close to one another so we decided to spend the day together. She wasn't feeling that well so I decided to visit her at home. I go into her house, lucky for me her parents had gone to the beach for the day, and see her lying on the living-room sofa with her eyes closed. She looked like a corpse, so I decided to go along with my fantasy and treat her like one.

I started to explain to her that I was a mortician and she was my corpse and that I was going to have my way with her. As I outlined the whole scenario, she lay there with her eyes closed and completely willing. I explained to her that I would first have to remove all of her clothes to see how she had died.

I unbuttoned her shirt and slid down her shorts, and she was completely naked under that. I began to touch and probe her body, running my fingers up and down the length of her. I told her I had seen a lot of dead bodies before but that I felt particularly bad that she was so young and wanted to make love to her. I opened her mouth and put my tongue inside but there was no response so I moved down her body.

I spread her legs open and put my tongue inside, flickering the lips of her vagina. I licked, tasted, and sucked on her wetness with my face completely submerged against the inside of her body.

With my tongue inside of her, I reached my hands up to her breasts and began to fondle them. The only sign I received that she was aroused was her erect nipples; aside from that she didn't flinch and kept her eyes closed the entire time.

I took my finger and put it inside her and her state of deadness aroused me so much that I started to stroke my penis up and down. I asked her, "Please revive from the dead, I need to fuck you," but there was no answer and no movement. I continued to jerk myself off aggressively, as a sweet fluid ran down her legs, and I began to lean over and lick it off. I took my hard-on and rubbed it against her thighs, begging her to have her way with me, but still there was no response. I opened her mouth and put my penis inside, lowering myself in and out of her, but that was not enough. I needed impact.

I told her that I needed to move her from the sofa because she was almost ready for viewing and makeup. I lifted her limp body and threw her over a chair by the window in the sunlight. I told her that first I was going to clean her insides. She lay on her stomach over the chair with her arms hanging to the floor and her legs wide open. I took the cleaning tool, my penis, and shoved it into her from behind. Her limp body was the victim to my intense fucking. I needed to revive her, I wanted her to fuck me back. I took my finger and stimulated her clit, while my penis tore into her like a blowtorch.

Finally, as she sensed my body trembling for hers, she threw me down and sat down on my bulging, throbbing hard-on and fucked me like a whore in the night. I grabbed her breasts with force and rocked her back and forth on my penis, till I came like a waterfall inside of her. I took her in my arms and squeezed her real tight . . . it was great to have her back from the dead!

Dirty Dancing

"Les" is twenty-seven years old, owns a modeling agency and lives in Los Angeles.

I see this girl in an extremely crowded club—the type of place with lights flashing and the bass so loud that you can't hear yourself think, the type of place where actions speak louder than words and eye contact means underlying desire.

I make my way over to her and she starts to dance in front of me extremely seductively, trying to make me respond. She rubs against the front of my body, putting direct pressure on my hard-on, and then moves behind me. She wraps her arms around my waist and pushes her pelvis into my ass, grinding along with the beat of the music.

As the intensity of the bass picks up, I swing her around and shove my tongue down her throat. I take my hands and slide them under her miniskirt. She has garters attached to her stockings, but her vagina is exposed. I enter the hole that is public to me and slide my fingers into her. She becomes limp in my arms and starts to squat up and down so that I can penetrate her deeper. She starts to suck on my neck as she moans in my ear from the stimulation that I am giving her. As I am fingering her, she is rubbing my hard-on, which is about to burst out of my pants. People are rubbing against us on the dance floor and are watching attentively. I love the attention and she is wrapped up in her pleasure so that she doesn't notice or care. She sticks her hand in my pants and starts to stroke me up and down. Blood rushes to my penis and I need to be inside her. I turn her around, lift up her skirt and ram my penis inside her. I swing my hand to the front and rub her clit at the same time. My penis is swimming in her juices and my balls are slapping her ass like a dominatrix would whip her subject.

I push my hands up her body and underneath her shirt. I take her breasts in my hands and start to twist her hard nipples forcefully. The impact is not good enough . . . I grab her by the waist and push the top portion of her body down so that she is hanging over my arm. As I push my penis in deeper and deeper, she swings on my arm like a chimp. I take my foot and move her feet apart, spreading her legs so wide that I can rip right through her.

People on the dance floor are responding to us . . . two women start to touch each other as they watch us. I make eye contact with them as my hard-on is getting attended to and one of them opens the other one's shirt and starts to suck on her huge milky breasts, literally shoving them whole into her mouth.

This is visual enough to get me off but I won't let myself because it feels too good. As I watch the two women, one of them moves down and sticks her face up the other's skirt. I can't see her face but I can see the head moving about under the fabric and the woman who keeps bobbing her knees, lowering her cunt to be probed.

I get so crazy when I see this that I grab the girl I am fucking and lean her over the railing of the dance floor and bang my penis inside of her till my come explodes inside her. I turn her around and push her mouth down around my joystick till she sucks it clean while I watch the two women tongue fucking and fingering on the dance floor.

An Evening at the Mall

"Scott" is thirty-four years old. He is a technician for a TV station in Tulsa, Oklahoma. "I've been in my current relationship for two years," he says.

We meet anonymously at a shopping mall. She approaches me in front of a store window and begins to explain the sexual needs she has and how she would like me to fulfill them.

Some of the things she says go like this: "I want you to touch me all over and put yourself inside me. I want to feel your hard prick inside my body. I know that you could make me come so hard, please touch me now!"

With these words, I force her against the store window and start petting her and licking her all over. I run my hands over her breasts, moving them forcefully down her body, and massaging her vagina through her clothing.

"You think you're such a man?" she taunts me, as I look deeply into her eyes. "Well, then, show me. Fuck me now." I know what she wants but I want to tease her for a while. I don't want to give it up that easily. I slowly unzip her dress and slide it off her shoulders, and it falls around her ankles. She is not wearing any underwear. I lower my head and begin to lick along her inner thighs. She arches her back and widens her legs.

I take my hand and tickle her silky pubic hairs while I lick her thighs, and she is pushing my head toward her. I finally cave in because I want to taste her so badly and I slam my tongue into her vagina.

I move my tongue around, stimulating her clit and pinching her nipples with my fingers. She starts to pound up and down onto my face, literally fucking my mouth, making me crazily aroused. "If you want me to slide it in," I tell her, "you're going to have to suck it." She pulls my cock out of my pants and sticks the whole length inside of her mouth. She goes up and down with her mouth and strokes me with her hand simultaneously. She licks and sucks me until the veins of my prick start to bulge and I want to fuck the hell out of her.

I push her onto the ground and force my way in, slamming open the lips of her vagina. I push my head in between her breasts and suck the meat on them. I wrap my arms around her and turn on the floor so that she is on top of me. I reach my arms up to her breasts and begin to smack them around while she rides me like a rodeo champion. My hard-on is expanding inside of her and I'm about to explode.

I lift her off of me and turn her around for more impact. I pin her against the store window with her face suctioned against the glass. I take myself and get her from behind, with her vagina slapping against the glass. I'm fucking her so hard that her juices are dribbling down her thighs, and with one final thrust, I pour my semen inside her with thousands of spurts.

"Scott" provided us with a real sexual experience that lacks the public aspect of the fantasy while retaining the anonymity.

I was working in a restaurant as a waiter. I had on the typical uniform: black pants, a white shirt and a towel hanging off an apron string that smacked me in the ass every time I walked.

Anyway, this woman calls me over and says, "I love your toweletta." She made it quite clear that she was available and I knew that the evening would end in a nightcap. She

watched me seductively the entire evening as I served people their dinners and filled countless drink orders. She must
have been numb with boredom by the time we left together.

We get to my house hastily and start to rip off one another's clothes. She looks at me and says, "You have the perfect penis for my ass. Get on top of me and hump me till I'm
done and then I promise to please you back." That was
enough for me to be pleased, but I didn't question her and I
shoved my hard-on inside her, ramming it in with such
force that I thought I would cut her in half.

I reached around her and stimulated her clit at the same
time till she was screaming from the pleasure. She stood on
the side of the bed with the top portion of her body on the
bed and I stood behind her feeding her my beef. I needed to
suck her breasts and see her fuck me in order to get off, and
just when I had these thoughts, I began to fuck her so hard
that her come came bursting out all over the place.

I slid out my bouncing erection and she threw me onto
the floor, jumping on top of me. "Now, I'm going to fuck
you," she said. She began to rock back and forth onto my
prick as I smothered my face into her chest, sucking her
beautiful milk-filled breasts. They were so huge that I ate
them all up . . . I could not get enough of her. Suddenly she
brought her knees close together and put her arms around
them and began to jump up and down onto my dick, so that
every other stroke I would pull completely out of her and
plunge in again. After a moment, I forced her to sit down,
grabbing her hips and having her body grind against mine.

I could feel the wet lips of her vagina moving against me
and my penis swimming in her juices. She was the wettest
thing I had ever felt . . . after a few more moments of intense fucking, I had my come shot inside of her and she collapsed onto my chest. This fuck was definitely something!

• • •

Is there something else involved here? More than just a pragmatic compromise between the glands and the emotions? I think there is.

It relates to a phrase I used toward the beginning of this chapter— politically correct. I'd like to think that in the best of all possible worlds, sex would be the last thing to get run through the meat grinder of ideological orthodoxy. But I'm afraid it was among the first.

The sex-with-a-stranger fantasy may also be a reaction to attempts to edit and censor sex as if it were an ideological text, rather than an act of physical and emotional intimacy between adults. One-night stands and sex with strangers aren't "SC"—sexually correct. Yet when it comes to fantasy, men don't get it and I suspect they never will.

Men have had their behavior and the content of their characters analyzed in depth by authors and experts, talk show hosts and talk show guests, and magazine articles and newspaper columns for the better part of thirty years. Only the "Walkman" exceeds "Problem-man" as a consumer product that came out of nowhere and exploded into a zillion-dollar profit maker.

Male bashing has been lucrative and entertaining. Even its more benign form, male-pondering, has made its practitioners nice money. The big business of cultural war is hell, and there's been no escaping it. But there is a way out of sorts. This fantasy scenario that we've been discussing here amounts to Fort Apache. The place is surrounded and the garrison is holed up inside defiantly fantasizing about sex with strangers. If the PC and SC police don't like it—tough!

I could call it, instead of Fort Apache, the last all-male social club. But I think men know that such institutions are ultimately doomed. Even the metaphor won't survive much longer. But the fantasy will endure out on the frontier, behind the rough-hewn stockade of the male imagination.

Howdy, Ma'am. New in town?

Five

Secrets Purchased: Sex with Prostitutes

This chapter is all about having it both ways.

At the core of fantasies that feature sex with a prostitute is the need for the ultimate in control: He pays his money and gets what he wants. At the same time, though, the transaction hinges on giving up control. She takes the money and, in so doing, relieves him of the need to be in control.

Control without control.

The contradiction is fascinating. I think it perfectly captures the nature of the sexual split personality of many men. They want control but not the responsibility and consequences that are an organic part of it.

And who can blame them for that? Not me. I'm a man and know that being behind the wheel of the race car named desire is great fun but also, at times, a major burden. I'm not talking about the more cosmic aspects of the issue, either, like the care and feeding of relationships and all that. Just trying not to make a fool of yourself while maintaining control is hard enough. Then there's the challenge of satisfying your partner, a task that is never easy, given the nagging thought that she is lying there thinking, "Is this guy pathetic or what?"

To understand the fantasy we'll need to examine the reality. Over the years I've talked to men who have been involved with prostitutes and I've asked: Why?

Why, in an era when sex is freely available, does a man pay for it?

An answer—maybe not *the* answer—is that he is buying something more than sex; something that is not available in other forms.

When I look at these fantasies involving sex with prostitutes, I see several different agendas being followed in which the actual sex act is a secondary motive. The prostitute is cover—a net of camouflage concealing drives that are more central than having intercourse.

Basically, I think there are three of them:

1. performance anxiety;
2. performance anxiety; and,
3. performance anxiety.

There's more to it than fear of impotence or of being confronted with their own sexual mediocrity. Men are essentially buying peace of mind and buying themselves out of the physical and emotional obligations associated with sexual intimacy. This one-way commerce puts the burden back on the prostitute. Her client can smell bad, look bad, love bad. His money's good and that's enough.

Prostitution has survived as an occupation because the ladies of the night provide a product that other women can't match: an antidote to vulnerability. The price of sexual control is paid in hard currency, not in hard knocks. It is a transaction that purchases the ultimate Teflon coating. Nothing sticks, not even the truth.

At the same time, in many instances, validation is also part of the transaction. The prostitute's client buys self-esteem. Some of them will even try to make her come—what a man!

• • •

It used to be that brothels were seen as places where men went to obtain sex of a kind that they were not getting at home within a marriage. Fifty or so years ago, to most professional observers of sexual mores and practices, that meant oral sex, some milder forms of S&M and an uninhibited sexuality that, for some couples, wasn't considered proper.

Technically, in that case, the last bordello should have closed its doors around 1970. Oral sex and maybe what should be called freestyle sex have been the norm since then. But prostitutes are still in business because they offer men the right to be lousy lovers.

For fifty or a hundred dollars they don't have to worry about coming too soon, whether the foreplay is adequate or which one of their partner's erogenous zones needs attention. The prostitute is creating a bubble of comfort and security for her client.

Even better than the old business adage to sell "the sizzle not the steak," prostitutes are selling a vacuum.

The fantasies—and it's time to bail out of reality—expand the vacuum by allowing men to dispense with the prostitute. There's no need to actually visit a brothel or take a chance on doing a Hugh Grant and ending up in a starring role with the vice squad.

Here again the fantasy is a mechanism for achieving sexual satisfaction—or at least simulating it—without running the risks of actually living out the scenario. The fantasy functions as both medium and message. Invulnerability is the destination *and* the route of travel.

I'll start with "Harrison's" fantasy because it is perhaps the riskiest of them all in that the medium is prostitution and the message is incest. If there's anyone in need of a zone of invulnerability, it is a guy who entertains thoughts of sex with his sisters.

Sister Act

"Harrison," fifty-five years old, is a fine-arts appraiser. He lives in Richmond, Virginia.

I've never been to a massage parlor but I imagine going to one and spending an evening evaluating the women. I choose two for their beauty and personalities. I make them a proposition: I'll pay fifteen hundred dollars each and all expenses if they accompany me for a two-week vacation at a house my family has owned for years on the beach in North Carolina. They both agree and off we go.

Sonja and Betsy are their names. On the drive down there, I carefully explain the scenario in detail—I guess this is a fantasy within a fantasy—they are my sisters and after years of brotherly lust I am going to fuck them. When we arrive, I assign each of them to my real sisters' bedrooms in the house.

On the first night I visited Sonja. We only snuggled together under the covers and talked. Then I went to Betsy's room and did the same thing.

In some versions of the fantasy, this chastity business goes on for a few days, with the visits getting increasingly erotic. The one I use more often is this: After I leave Betsy to go back to my room to sleep, I stop on the front porch to have a smoke. As I'm admiring the full moon, the screen door that leads to the house opens and Sonja appears. She is naked and appears to be sleepwalking. She passes by me to lie down on the chaise longue. Her skin glistens in the moonlight. I come up behind her and gently reach around to touch her breasts. Sonja sighs contentedly. I kiss the top of her breasts and lean down and brush my lips against the nipples. From there I move to her stomach, thighs and pussy.

The back of the chaise longue is slightly reclined so that Sonja's head is near my crotch. She reaches up and pulls out my cock from the pajama bottoms that I'm wearing. She strokes it gently and kisses it. I swing around and straddle the chaise longue with my feet planted on either side. Sonja takes my cock in her mouth and kneads it with her lips and tongue.

She brings me to the brink of ejaculating, but I pull out and as I do so Sonja draws her knees toward her chest to make room for me on the lower end of the chaise. I sit down with my feet still on either side. Sonja throws her legs around my back and slides up onto my thighs, swinging her hips upward. She reaches down and inserts my prick into her.

For a moment we're still, caught in suspended animation, and then she begins to slowly pump. The rhythm gains force and speed as we rock back and forth and I bounce her on my thighs. As my ecstasy builds, I stand, picking her up with me and staying deep within. I'm in a half-crouch, supporting her with my hands under her ass, swinging my hips for penetration. Sonja has her head thrown back, moaning. Just as I'm about to let go, she reaches around and squeezes my balls. I can't come now and it drives me wild.

I back away from the chaise longue, spin around and throw her onto the top of the picnic table. I hammer away, gasping and twisting to get her to release my balls. She screams as I make a mighty thrust and lets go of my balls. I erupt into her.

We stay on top of the table in each other's arms for about ten minutes until Sonja squirms out from under me, gets up and leaves without a word. I have another cigarette and then go into bed but in passing Betsy's room, I decide to try for a doubleheader. I enter. She is lying on the bed on top of the covers, asleep. I lift the hem of her night dress above her hips to admire her pussy. I'm instantly hard again. I climb on top of her and slip it in.

She doesn't stir even as I pump and pump and pump. It

seems as if I have to work an hour to get off again. I finally come—and go.

The scenario repeats exactly each night for two weeks. I take Sonja and Betsy back to the massage parlor at the end of the two weeks and arrange for them to join me the following summer.

Obviously, I've got a thing for my sisters but I'd never have sex with them. The fantasy is always with two prostitutes who are about twenty years old, more than half of my sisters' current ages.

For Medicinal Purposes Only

"Maury," forty years old, is a lawyer from Boise, Idaho.

I've had a bad car accident, hit my head and am in a coma. Even so, I can see and hear. I just can't move or speak. I'm in a nursing home and one day my best friend Jim notices that as the nurse bathes me I get a hard-on. He has an idea.

The next evening he arrives with a hooker. When the coast is clear, they pull back the covers and she massages my balls. Coma or not, I immediately stand up straight. The whore blows me, takes her money and leaves.

A few days later, Jim brings another prostitute. This time, she climbs on top of me and rides till I come. Over the next few weeks, Jim brings several other hookers to provide this "therapy." He tells me, not knowing that I can hear, that it is "the least I can do."

One night, Jim has a hooker with him and his girlfriend,

Lynn. Together they watch the pro do her thing and I notice that Jim's girl is discreetly rubbing his crotch while I am being treated.

When the prostitute leaves, Jim's girl approaches the bed and examines me. I'm only wearing a T-shirt. "Nice dick," she says. "Too bad about the accident."

My hard-on is beginning to shrink but she reaches out and strokes it. "Do you think he knows what's going on," she asks?

"No, the doctors say he's a vegetable," Jim replies.

With that, Lynn climbs onto the bed, straddling me. She hikes her skirt, slides down her pantyhose and panties and wedges me inside of her.

Lynn worked very slowly, back and forth, enjoying the pleasure. Jim moves to the head of the bed and watches her get off. After that, Lynn starts visiting me once or twice a week and bringing a few of her girlfriends along. And I live happily ever after.

Room Service

"Walt," twenty-six years old, is a roofing contractor in Portland, Maine. He's married with two little boys. "I've had this fantasy since way before I was married and living in Boston," he says.

I'm between girlfriends—way between. My sexual needs are rising like the sap in springtime so I pick up a good-looking hooker at a downtown hotel. We go up to a room that I arranged for in advance. I tell her to take off her clothes, which she does slowly with discreet but sexy flair. I run a tub full of warm water with lots of bubble bath and motion for her to get in. I take off my own clothes but instead of joining her I kneel on the tile bathroom floor and wash her like a baby.

I towel her dry and lead her to the bed. Over the next half-hour I give her a deep massage. My fingers gently work her over from head to foot. In fact, as I finish with her toes and the soles of her feet, she rolls over onto her back and spreads her legs wide.

I accept the invitation and we make love passionately but without a lot of gymnastics. There's a tenderness as we do it in the classic missionary position. She climaxes just before I do. I hold her in my arms until we drop off to sleep.

In a few hours I feel her get out of bed. There's enough light from the bathroom that I can watch her dress. She's a beautiful thing.

As she moves to the door, I say, "What do I owe you?"

In reply, she just blows me a kiss and leaves.

Permission Granted

"Shad," thirty-eight years old, is a physical therapist, based in Provo, Utah. He wrote me to say that he and his wife, a registered nurse, believe strongly in having open, healthy sexual relationships.

I'm at a conference in a city about two hours from home. I figure that it might not be a bad time to check out the local women. My wife, Debbie, had told me that if I met someone while I was away and was attracted to her I was to go ahead and have a night of fun, as long as I told her everything that went on.

Well, I try the bar and it is dead. And I mean dead. I ask the bartender where the action is and she suggests a place nearby that is known for good times and good women. I go over there but it's just as bad.

When I get back to the motel at about 11:00 P.M. I remember that when I worked in the area for a few weeks at one point, I saw ads for escort services in the Yellow Pages. I take a look and bingo! There must be fifteen ads. I pick a few and call. The first says there is only one woman working my area and that she is tied up until 1:00 A.M. That's too late. I try another but there's no one available there, either. A third call turns up a guy who wants to know what kind of woman I want. I've always had this thing for redheads, so that's what I tell him. He says the one redhead is busy and asks for another preference, and I say "brunette," which does the trick. He tells me that Tina will call me back.

About twenty minutes later I get the call. She has the sexiest voice I've ever heard. I ask how much and she says $175 for a lingerie show and some hugging and kissing. If I want anything more it will cost me a "tip." I ask what a $50 tip would get me. Tina said she'd do something for me but for $100 I'd get the "whole package."

She arrives a little later, looking very smart and not like a call girl at all. Tina is beautiful and small, with small tits—which I like. We discuss money. I tell her that I've never done anything like this and am extremely nervous. She smiles and counts out the money I hand her: $275 for the "whole package."

She goes to the phone to check in with her answering service and confirm that the deal is transpiring.

She wastes no time after that. She asks if I want her to get into some lingerie that she brought with her. From her overnight bag, she produces two teddies, very sexy and sheer, from Victoria's Secret. I nod my approval of her lingerie and when I look up she is taking off her coat and unbuttoning her blouse. She turns around and takes off the top and then her pants, puts her heels back on and faces me. Tina is a vision of beauty. She has on a white bra and panty set, with thigh-high stockings and about four-inch white heels.

My cock springs to instant attention as I look at her. She comes over to me and takes off my sweater and unbuckles my pants. I step back and remove my shoes and socks and then take off the rest of my clothes down to my silk boxers. Tina says she loves my choice of underwear.

We chat and I discover that Tina is a really nice person. We have a lot in common. I tell her that I'm married, which shocks her, but it's all right after we talk about Debbie for a few minutes.

We then go to bed. We cuddle and hug for a little bit and then she begins to feel me. I take off her bra and begin to caress her small but firm breasts. I lick and suck on them for a while and then she goes to work and takes off my shorts and begins to give me head. She's an excellent cocksucker and has me on the brink of orgasm quite a few times, but I never go over the edge.

I reach down and take her head away from my dick because I'm afraid I will let go and the "whole package" will be over too soon. I ask her to come back up and cuddle and play with me for a while. I kiss her at that point. Now I have always heard that prostitutes did not kiss their clients, so I'm surprised when she kisses me back passionately. It's a great kiss.

I ask her if anyone had ever pleased her sexually. She says that she's here for me, not her. I ask in reply what if pleasing me meant pleasing her—taking care of her needs—would that make a difference? She asks what I had in mind. I tell her more cuddling, fingering her and maybe eating her out. She agrees, and I can't believe it!

Tina spreads out on the bed and opens her legs for me. I take off her panties slowly with my teeth, kissing my way up and down her thighs and calves as the panties come down. She's getting turned on by this and moans. Then I spread her open and lick her, slowly at first. I go up one lip and down the other, staying away from the clit for now. She begins to lubricate some, and then a lot, so I go for the clit. She jumps a little and then moans loudly and begins to really move her hips.

I have a hard time keeping up with her but I manage. I insert two fingers inside of her beautiful pussy and find her G-spot. Despite what some so-called experts say, it does exist, and Tina and Debbie have them! As if to verify the location, Tina begins to lubricate on my fingers, and I can tell that she is close to an orgasm.

I then put my mouth on her clit and suck it in gently between my lips, increasing the pressure and adding flicks of my tongue back and forth until she comes. While she gushes, Tina is yelling, "Damn you, damn you, damn you . . . this is not the way it's supposed to be!" When she recovers I ask her about the outburst and she says that I was supposed to get the pleasure. I tell her that it pleased me to make her come and she thanks me with another passionate kiss, and then puts a condom on me and gets on top and rides my cock like there was no tomorrow. It doesn't take me long to come.

We get up to clean off and since I have time left on the meter we lie back on the bed and I cuddle her and we talk about fifteen minutes. She checks with her service while she's still naked and in my arms and I think she would stay all night if she could. She kisses me again and tells me she has to get going.

She gets dressed and we talk about maybe having a three-some with Debbie. Tina says she's all for it, if I make the offer right. I ask her how much, and she says if she likes what I have planned, she'll do it for free.

As a postscript to "Shad's" fantasy, he told us that the basic elements of the scenario actually happened and the event provided him with the raw material for this fantasy and variations on it. Shad said that he and his wife will act out the fantasy, pretending that Debbie is hidden in the room watching as Tina and her husband make love. Debbie enjoys the fantasy as much as "Shad." According to him, she masturbated three times as he told her about the original incident.

In terms of sheer numbers, fantasies involving prostitutes aren't as common as some other recurring themes. I suspect that's because the reality of prostitution is so powerful and, in many ways, repulsive.

Nelson Algren, who wrote *The Man with the Golden Arm,* advocated following three rules: "Never play cards with a man named Doc, never eat in a place called Mom's, and never sleep with a woman whose problems are worse than your own." I think men are unconsciously following rule three by choosing less troubling fantasy scripts that feature women whose major problems center on achieving the perfect orgasm (with them).

Most men would acknowledge that prostitutes, even those they have had contact with in real life, are usually grappling with big-time problems. Even if there is such a creature as the "happy hooker," there's a general suspicion that orgasms are not all that she's faking.

Another factor is that the prostitute fantasy is one that can be easily acted out. "If you've got the money, honey . . ." The most attractive fantasies are those that hover just beyond reach. They're both possible and impossible. With these fantasies, feasibility can be confirmed any night of the week by a cruise through a big city's red-light district (small, medium and suburbs, too).

Yet, the theme that underpins this fantasy is nonetheless valid. Finding an antidote to the sense of vulnerability is a real male need, so real it transforms itself into fantasy, and as such it is providing a double layer of protection: One, the act really isn't happening, and two, even the imaginary situation is guilt-free because it involves an exchange of money.

Fantasies are always there as a safety net, even if it means bending Nelson Algren's third rule.

Part II

Taboo Breaking

Six

Secrets of Triangles: The Classic Ménage à Trois

If I had organized this book to present male fantasies in order of prevalence—most frequent themes to least frequent—I would have begun with the classic ménage à trois. Far and away, it's the favorite.

In the sprawling male theme park of fantasy sex, making love to two women at the same time is the star attraction and, with the exception of the confident woman, everything else is sort of Mickey Mouse by comparison.

I think the appeal is pretty basic: If having sex with one woman is terrific, sex with two women must be twice as nice.

Psychologist Carol Friedland, with whom I discussed the phenomenon, had a more complicated take on it, though. She said the ménage à trois's appeal as a fantasy relates to its primary attraction as an actual erotic act: It relieves men of the need to interact emotionally and verbally during sex. They've either got their hands full satisfying two women or are busy watching as the women satisfy each other. Sharing feelings or uttering words of more than one syllable are not necessary.

I buy that, along with the notion that the ménage à trois is the ultimate confident-woman fantasy, offering great sex, shared power, less constricting roles and no rejection.

Most ménage à trois fantasies allow men to be the center of attention and desire at any given moment or to move off to the side to enjoy the show. There's research that indicates that visual stimulation causes male testosterone levels to rise, and therefore this urge to step back and play spectator may have a biological function. It also helps explain, if Dr. Friedland is right, about the link between testosterone levels and verbal acuity—why many men turn into the "strong, silent type" during sex.

Let's not kid ourselves. For a dehydrated male ego, a ménage à trois fantasy is like chugging a bucket full of Gatorade (with a testosterone chaser). He is getting a huge dose of confirmation of his sexual desirability.

As fantasies go, "MAT" offers a maximum amount of stimulation and entertainment and minimal emotional conflict and ambivalence. A man doesn't have to make lame excuses to himself to justify fifteen minutes daydreaming about being in the sack with two women. He's a stud—a legend in his own mind—doing what comes naturally for any self-respecting sexual thoroughbred.

There are any number of fantasies where that is certainly not the case. Masturbatory fantasies, to name one, which we will focus on later in the book, are loaded with deep-seated misgivings about the biblical taboo of "spilling thy seed on barren ground."

Yet, there is a taboo quality to the ménage à trois that makes the thought of breaking it exciting and dangerous. Never underestimate the pleasure of thumbing your nose at convention. Put something off-limits and it immediately becomes an object of desire. Most of the MAT fantasies involve one man and two women—Naughty. The women often have sex with each other—Very Naughty.

I think this is a special case of vicarious taboo breaking. It's about as close as many men will ever come to a homoerotic fantasy. The women are safe surrogates. They can have sex with each other, he can watch and there's no danger of having to confront his own longings, curiosity, interest—whatever—in the act of physical intimacy between two people of the same sex. In short, he doesn't have to wonder, "Am I gay?"

On the other hand, a fantasy about a wife or girlfriend having sex with another women doesn't necessarily lead to the thought that "my wife is a lesbian." Women have permission from society for more physical contact with each other than men do. It's okay to dance, hold hands, kiss or hug. There's no suggestion of homosexuality. Likewise, the sex in a ménage à trois fantasy tends to get shrugged off as a relatively harmless form of heavy petting or feeds a male conceit that it was his sexual magic power that conjured up the whole thing. They're heterosexual but couldn't help themselves once the "Merlin of the Mattress" waved his wand.

If nothing else the ménage à trois fantasies in this chapter confirm the old truth that for every kid, there's a candy story.

Out of the Closet

"Barry" is forty-one and lives in Carlsbad, California. He's a general contractor, married twenty years with three children.

I have many fantasies, and why not? Nobody has to know about them. This is my favorite one. It's the middle of the night and my wife wakes me up by putting her hands in my boxer shorts and rubbing my penis. She starts to kiss me and takes my hand and pushes it down her body. I know what she wants. She whispers in my ear, "If you please me now,

I'll have a surprise for you." I think it's some new dildo, or gadget, no big deal, but I please her anyway because I love to see her eyes roll up into her head.

She arches her back and pushes her body down so that my fingers penetrate her even deeper. I feel her wetness, and she pulls me up so that I can slide into her. She feels so good. She's so wet that I can't control myself anymore, and I come inside her. I pull out and lie on my back, and she rests her head on my chest with her leg wrapped around my waist. She whispers, "Wait here, I have something for you."

She goes to the closet, which is already slightly open, and pushes the clothing to one side, and there it is—her best friend is standing there in a red, lacy teddy, touching herself, and fully aroused. I get an immediate hard-on. My wife leads her to the bed holding her hand, and she comes and lies down next to me.

She looks at me and says, "Touch me." I look at my wife for her permission, and she says, "What do you think I brought her here for?" At this point her friend is completely stimulating herself. I take her hand out and push my fingers all the way in. She is moaning as if she has never been touched before. At the same time, my wife has my penis in her mouth, but I need impact. I take her friend and turn her around and I'm driving it in from the rear. My wife is under her friend and is sucking her breasts and stimulating her clitoris at the same time. She is screaming from the pleasure. After her friend and I come to a crazy climax, my wife needs more. She wraps her legs around my neck and puts her wetness on my face. I use my tongue as a probe to tease and push her. After my wife's juices run down my face, the three of us intertwine ourselves and fall into a numbing sleep.

•   •   •

As for hot sex experiences from real life, "Barry" offered one with a much, much lower temperature than usual. It makes for an interesting and telling comparison with the fantasy.

Well, if you knew my wife, you'd know that hot sex is not really her thing. Heck, sex isn't really her thing. My wife's philosophy about sex sounds something like this . . . get in, get out, get off, get to sleep. She doesn't communicate what she wants and she won't use me as a play toy, the way I want to be used. At times, she even thinks that I'm perverted, but there was one night that was different, a night that the sex wasn't real great, but real good anyway.

It was a couple of weeks after we got married. We borrowed her parents' house in the mountains for the weekend. After a lengthy dinner on the deck and two bottles of wine, she came and sat on my lap. I started kissing her neck. I untucked her shirt and moved my hand up to her breast and started rubbing it. She pushed her head all the way back . . . she was enjoying it.

I stood up with her in my arms and I lay her on the hard deck floor. I undid the buttons on her skirt, one by one, and became immediately aroused. After her clothes were off, I lay down and pulled her on top of me. I was still fully clothed, but I wanted her to feel how hard I was and help me take everything off.

I pulled her back and forth by the hips, and she began to increase the friction. My clothing was not allowing her to get the feeling she wanted, she wanted my flesh. She unzipped my pants and helped me pull them off. I pulled her up and slid right into her. She started rocking so hard that the wood floor was scraping my back like a knife, but I enjoyed the pain. I grabbed her hips, clenched them and helped her to move faster and faster. It was a riding the crest feeling for both of us.

She came first, and then a couple of moments later, I did. This memory dates back about nineteen years. It hasn't been the same since. It doesn't seem as if she enjoys sex anymore, and how can I enjoy it if my partner acts as if she is doing me a favor?

Sight Unseen

"John" is fifty-one. He lives in Vineland, New Jersey, and works in a bank's marketing and promotion department. His current marriage has lasted twelve years, precisely as long as the first.

My fantasies usually revolve around oral sex and bondage. I enjoy a little pain and I love to be "tied and teased." My ultimate fantasy is this: My wife ties me up to the bedpost . . . so tight that the rope is cutting into my wrists. She then proceeds to blindfold me. I feel her breath on my body but she is not touching me. She teases me with this heat for a while until I feel a hot liquid seep down my thighs . . . it's milk. She's licking it off me.

At this moment, I hear the bedroom door open. I say, "Who's there?" But no one answers. My wife starts kissing me to tame my curiosity. I feel another person climb onto the bed. My wife continues to kiss me as I feel a tongue on my penis . . . licking me, sucking me . . . all of a sudden the pleasure stops . . . my wife and the stranger get off the bed . . . I hear the moaning of two women . . . the stranger asks my wife, "Should I go deeper? Show me what you like."

I hear them pleasing one another, humping one another . . . the sound sends blood rushing to my penis . . . I want to touch myself but I can't . . . I'm all tied up . . . I hear the sound of bodies moving, tongues licking . . . I'm going crazy . . . after a prolonged agony of ten minutes they both climb onto the bed. One sits on my face . . . allowing me to feel the wetness of her pleasures. The other one sits on my penis and starts rocking.

They are moving toward one another . . . rocking me, touching each other, and doing everything they can to make me climax. It's my fantasy, so it takes me a while to come . . . I keep holding it in . . . it hurts, but it feels so good . . . they are riding me so hard my wrists begin to bleed from the rope . . . "Harder," I say, "harder, harder," and I come unwillingly. The stranger gets off the bed and leaves the room. I have no idea who she was. I guess phenomenal sex involves mystery!

Potboiler

"John's" hot sex experience also involves his wife:

I was with my wife up in New Hampshire during a weekend getaway. The night began smoking marijuana. We had never smoked together. We were lying down on a rug, surrounded by the warmth of a fireplace. I began to touch her. Her breasts had never felt softer. I started to kiss her on the mouth, stomach, belly button . . . I undid the zipper on her pants and put my hands in between her creamy thighs.

She arched her back and moved her hips closer to me . . . I pushed my fingers deep in . . . she wrapped her legs around my head . . . she wanted full penetration . . . she pulled me up and started to kiss me . . . she maneuvered her hand between our bodies and began to squeeze my penis . . . rubbing it, squeezing it. She said, "Please put yourself inside me." I unbutton my fly and she jumps on top of me and begins to ride me. My pants aren't even off yet and the zipper is cutting into me, but I don't mind . . . she feels so good and she's so wet. I started to mold her nipples in my hands . . . she clawing my hips, holding, grinding me . . . she says to me "I want it from behind . . . hard."

I flip her round and drive it in. The marijuana had heightened every thrust and every touch. I grab her hips and pull her closer and closer, until I go pouring into her. We lie by the warmth of the fire naked all night long in each other's arms.

In his fantasy "John's" bonds and blindfold absolve him of responsibility. He doesn't object at all to the arrangement and obviously enjoys it. But he's designed a fantasy that really gets him off the hook for dreaming up a scenario that puts his wife in bed with another woman. And he doesn't even have to feel bad about watching—he can't see what's going on.

It's the great thing about fantasy. You get to change the names and details to protect the innocent.

If we consider "John's" real-life sexual encounter—also with his wife—there's another important aspect of the ménage à trois that comes into range. When another person (or persons) is involved in sex, the old adage is true: "Many hands make light work." On his own, "John" is getting a real workout. As erotic as it is, he's putting in hard, manual labor. It's easy to overlook that great sex is greatly demanding physically. The MAT turns it into something akin to tag-team wrestling. There's someone else available to step in and give you a breather.

A lot of men tell me that they worry about being able to "deliver the goods." They're anxious about ejaculating too soon or not being able to bring their partners to climax. The ménage à trois fantasy is a means of alleviating the anxiety.

A Friend in Need

"Carl" is in his mid-thirties. He's college-educated, white and single. Home is Everett, Washington. He told us he's had a lot of experience with prostitutes. "Carl" said he's slept with about fifty-five women, mostly hookers, after losing his virginity in a legal brothel in Nevada at the age of eighteen. But fear of AIDS and other diseases has shifted his focus to meeting women in more everyday situations.

> *Like* many men, I have often thought of having sex with more than one woman. My fantasy involves a former girl-friend and one of her friends. I come home from work and "Gina" and her friend "Carol" are relaxing on my couch, talking and watching TV. They've been drinking but are not drunk. We exchange "hellos" and I go straight to the kitchen and grab a cold beer. In the other room I hear them giggling but don't think much of it and go upstairs. After a few minutes I go back down and upon entering the room they immediately stop talking. I ask Gina what's going on but she just smiles and looks first at Carol and then back at me and says "Nothing."
>
> Then they start giggling again and whispering so that I can't hear them. I walk over to the couch and sit down between them, and they seem to like that. Gina and Carol have known each other for several years and are close friends. Gina tells me that Carol hasn't "gotten any" since she broke up with her boyfriend five months earlier. Carol is some-what shocked that Gina has let the cat out of the bag but is

still able to laugh about it. Gina puts her arm around me and snuggles closer. Soon she is kissing me, at first softly and then passionately.

My first thought: Is this appropriate in front of Carol? To my surprise Gina keeps on kissing me while Carol doesn't say anything but watches both of us. Gina then reaches for my lap and rubs my penis through my pants. I'm feeling somewhat uncomfortable and embarrassed with Carol watching, but at the same time I feel excited by this voyeuristic situation. I casually ask Gina what she's doing and she answers, "I want you, right here, right now." "What about Carol?" I ask. "I think she wants to watch," she says. Carol looks at us and slowly nods in approval. At this point I need no further encouragement. I take off my clothes, Gina does the same. Gina is now naked and sprawled out on the couch and Carol is sitting fully clothed on the other couch directly opposite.

I am nude, standing over Gina with a semierect penis, and I'm sure, the dumbest look on my face. But I don't care. "Eat my pussy," Gina commands. I oblige her as always, and for the next ten minutes have my face buried between her legs. I love going down on Gina. In fact, I love going down on any woman. Always have, always will. I consider myself a connoisseur of cunnilingus. Gina and I have a great sex life and have tried every position imaginable, so it doesn't surprise me when she asks me to lick her butt also. She then turns over onto her stomach and assumes her favorite position.

I'm more than happy to provide this pleasure to my mate. We've done this many times before. I totally forget about our "guest" until I hear Carol exclaim, "Oh, my God!" as I go about probing Gina's asshole with my tongue. I look over and see Carol fingering herself, obviously enjoying the scene she is witnessing. Gina slowly looks over her shoulder at

Carol and says, "You can watch or you can join us. One is more fun than the other." Carol replies but I don't understand what she is saying under her breath. Soon all of her clothes are shed. Gina tells me that she wants Carol and that I should watch. I concur and am treated to a visual feast. They begin by softly kissing and hugging. Then the kisses become deeper and more passionate. Through their fumbling and giggling it's obvious that the experience is new to both of them.

Carol throws her head back and Gina begins licking and sucking her breasts. Her breathing becomes deeper and the moaning louder. They stop giggling and anticipate each other's touch. Gina suggests a mutually satisfying position and Carol eagerly agrees. They entwine in the 69 position with Carol on top. They greedily devour each other for what seems like an hour, although it is only for a few minutes. I want a closer look and walk over to the couch. I lean over and see Gina smile at me from under Carol's sexy body. I ask Gina if Carol tastes as good as she looks and she replies, "Go ahead and see for yourself."

I waste no time in licking Carol's ass and wet pussy. Gina smiles and I kiss her open mouth. We continue until Carol peers over her shoulder and mentions that she wants me inside her.

Gina makes a move to get out from underneath but Carol instructs her to stay—she wants Gina and me to pleasure her at the same time. Now I kneel down between them, Carol in the doggy style position with Gina underneath her so as to have access to Carol's pussy and to give Gina my balls. As I enter Carol the feeling is indescribable. I'm so used to being inside of Gina that the sensation of Carol is new and different. It is this moment that I savor, and I thrust into Carol time and time again with unparalleled lust. It's not long before I feel the familiar stirring in my loins and know I will come soon.

I pull out of Carol's pussy and rest the tip of my cock on the soft fleshy part that separates Carol's asshole and pussy: all the while Gina is slowly licking my balls. I spread Carol's ass cheeks so that I have a better view. What a turn-on! I can't hold back any longer and ejaculate with spurt after spurt. My come drips down and off Carol's engorged lips and into Gina's waiting mouth. I'm totally spent. The girls, however, are not done. Carol climbs off of Gina and kisses her passionately. They share my most intimate love juice and hug and kiss some more. I watch them for a while longer and I'm treated to seeing them orgasm at the same time.

After it's over we talk about what's just happened and agree that it was a lot of fun. Whether it will happen again no one knows, but it is something we all wanted to experience. I leave it at that.

Gina has told me before that she wanted to try another woman. But I never thought the other woman would be someone we know. It should be said that I never had any sexual thoughts of Carol before. Yes, she's attractive but I never fantasized about her and Gina together. I am not disappointed.

Carl supplied this postscript:

Bob, this is my most often recurring fantasy and I hope you can use it in your book. Some day I hope to live out such a fantasy and when I do I will feel that I have reached another sexual level.

The best part of this fantasy is that it is unpremeditated and spontaneous. If the situation I described had been planned by Gina and me I don't think it would have had the same impact and excitement. I may be wrong but that is my gut instinct. I have had many true sexual experiences but that is for another letter. Thank you for allowing me to share this with you.

The Dinner Party

"Andrew" is forty-nine. A business consultant, he lives near Akron, Ohio, a place he describes as "the city where the rubber used to meet the road."

This is a "might-have-been" fantasy, which is not an unusual genre for me since I've always tended to chicken out just when things started looking interesting.

I lived with a woman for several years. Ann was her name. The sex was okay but not great. One night we were having dinner at our place with a single girlfriend of Ann's, a dark-haired Italian-American with large breasts and a good figure (a little on the chunky side).

After we'd had several glasses of wine, Julie, our guest, started to complain about her sex life. She wasn't getting enough. There were suggestive jokes and the conversation continued in that same vein. Julie and Ann were getting high.

At one point, Julie was criticizing the sexual prowess of her last date and actually "borrowed" me to demonstrate a move he had attempted with her. I found myself on the couch with her in some sort of modified doggy position— our clothes were on—re-enacting the moment.

Ann sat by the table chuckling lewdly at the scene.

After we had dessert and it was getting late, Julie just

popped the question: "Why don't the three of us just go up-stairs and screw?"

So far the story is true. I liked the idea a lot and so did Ann, I think. But I did some kind of fast tap-dancing. I pre-tended she was just kidding. I think I was worried about making a fool of myself trying to satisfy two women.

Julie took the hint and went home. I've fantasized an al-ternative scenario ever since:

We go upstairs to the bedroom where I, first, slowly un-dress Ann as Julie watches. I leave her panties on, though. Then, I take off Julie's clothes, leaving her panties on, too. I get both women to stand on either side of me in front of the full-length mirror. I have my arms around them fondling a breast in each hand.

Julie unbuckles my belt and Ann unzips my fly. She reaches in and pulls out my cock, which immediately in-flates. The two women take turns stroking me. I watch in the mirror. Julie goes down on me. She takes my penis into her mouth and swallows it deeply and starts sliding her lips up and down the shaft. Ann, meanwhile, has her tongue in my mouth.

Julie reaches over and slips her hand inside my girl-friend's panties and inserts two fingers into her vagina. Ann softly sighs.

To keep from coming, I step back from the two of them, and Julie turns her full attention to Ann. She kisses her stomach and probes deeper into the vagina. I come around behind Ann and pull down her panties, exposing her lovely ass. Julie buries her face in Ann's pussy.

I'm holding Ann's breasts from behind and sliding my penis up and down through the valley of her buttocks. Julie reaches between Ann's legs and takes my cock and guides it into Ann from behind. Ann and I swing around so that we are facing the mirror that is attached to a large antique armoire. She holds on to its sides, and I pump away, clutching her hips for leverage.

Julie comes up behind me and gently massages and licks my balls.

In real life it would have been all over quickly. But this isn't real and I pull out of Ann, turning to face Julie, who is kneeling. She takes my penis in her mouth again and slowly bends over backward until her back is on the floor and her knees are bent, feet flat on the floor. I'm forced to crouch over her face with my cock between her teeth, balancing on my hands as if I'm about to do a handstand or a somersault. Ann starts licking my ass and then goes to work on Julie's crotch, ripping off the panties.

Julie is the one to gasp this time, and as she opens her mouth she releases my penis. I stand up to get out of the awkward position. Ann slides up and over Julie's body and the women writhe like two snakes. I join them. It's like a tag-team wrestling match. First, I have intercourse with Ann. We grind and hump for a minute. I pull out and slam into Julie. Again, there is humping and grinding. And so it goes, back and forth between the two women.

Ann climaxes first. She shudders and moans. I pull out without coming and enter Julie, who is on her back, legs spread. Good old missionary position. We take our time. It's almost slow motion. Julie comes with a flood. A dam bursting. As I let go, I can feel Ann kissing my back tenderly.

Given the popularity of the classic ménage à trois fantasy, you'd think it would be the one that gets acted out the most often. But I have a hunch that's not the case.

For all of its appeal, there are also danger zones that many men are conscious of and avoid. As "Andrew" suggested in the prelude to his fantasy, what if he's not able to satisfy two women? Or what if she likes her better than him?

In some ways, the ménage à trois fantasy works better as fiction than nonfiction.

Of all the erotic options that are open to adults, the ménage à trois—and other group arrangements—makes me nervous. It has the potential to do great damage to a couple's relationship.

What seemed like such a great idea at the time can have unimagined negative effects. Relationships are built on trust, and while there are many that can and do survive a ménage à trois, there are at least an equal number, and I suspect far more, that would be severely damaged.

"Why did we do it?" "Should we do it again?" "Will he (or she) see her on the side." "Am I gay or bisexual?" These are thorny questions that can sap the strength of a relationship.

But if a ménage à trois happens, keep in mind that it was a joint decision.

Read that again—joint decision. That's what all good sex is about. It is a mutual undertaking. If there are misgivings and doubts, just move on. Assessing blame or indulging in guilt trips isn't the answer. Don't hesitate to seek professional counseling. A well-trained, experienced and neutral third party can help.

I'm not through with the ménage à trois fantasy. In the next chapter I'll offer several more that have a different context, involving two men and a woman. This is the reason I've been referring to the "classic ménage à trois." The mix of sexes makes for an important distinction. Perhaps these others should be called the fémage à trois fantasies. Aside from the fractured French, however, that's misleading in that it suggests that the female is central to the arrangement, which is an unlikely proposition. Clearly, the threesome's dynamics are altered—to say the least—as are the implications.

Seven

Secret Fears:
One Woman, Two Men
and a Bed

Most of the five hundred or so men whom I surveyed for this book would probably describe themselves as straight. I didn't make any effort to filter out gay or bisexual men, but my association with CNBC's *Real Personal,* which mostly focuses on heterosexual relationships, tended, in all likelihood, to attract respondents who were similarly inclined.

Having said that, I think the fantasies in this chapter are particularly interesting for the light they shed on the heterosexual male attitude toward sexuality that falls into a gray area that is neither straight, nor gay, nor "bi."

Fantasies are the perfect vehicle for exploring our erotic "back country." We can get off the road and take a close look at some rugged terrain that would be too dangerous to traverse on foot. Fantasies are totally deniable. In an instant, if things get out of hand, they can be stripped of all meaning and forgotten.

But there's another layer of protection in these fantasies. Rather than being fantasies about a mano-a-mano gay sexual encounter, the scenarios are crafted to lower the intensity of the shock waves that would be generated by having two men in the same bed together. Involving a woman in the equation, in effect acting as a mediator, is far less threatening than it would be to directly fantasize about a tryst with another man.

This raises the possibility that the fantasy mechanism is not as unencumbered by doubts and conflicts and role dissonance as might be presumed at first. If men are editing their fantasies, the parts that get left out are as important as those they include.

By red penciling homoerotic fantasies, cutting or repackaging them, men are demonstrating how uneasy—I can even say fearful—they are about the whole issue of homosexuality.

But I don't regard that as a big surprise. Just from the standpoint of the potential social sanctions that can be brought to bear, even idle intellectual curiosity about homosexuality cannot be indulged in lightly. Men who openly declare a gay or bisexual preference pay an enormous price. The rest of us know that and tread lightly, discreetly or not at all around the subject.

The fantasies in this chapter are examples of the light and discreet variety of footwork. I did not ask these men if they regarded themselves as gay or bisexual as a result of having the fantasies. Should I have? No. It was none of my business.

I think it would be a major mistake to read into these fantasies any meaning other than what I suggested above. Forget the word "latent." That a guy attends the opera every now and then doesn't mean that he desires to be Luciano Pavarotti.

The fantasies represented here are doing their job: allowing men to visit imaginary worlds and live imaginary lives.

This is Disney World for adults.

Chemical
Reaction

"Conner" is a thirty-three-year-old lawyer, living in Wichita, Kansas. This reads like a real-life sexual experience, but it was given to me as a fantasy.

My friend and I met a girl and had an affair for a week long. I enjoyed sharing a girl and being with my best friend at the same time.

She was from out of town and was staying at this motel, and my friend and I went over every second we could, if not together, alone. But every day would end with the three of us. When the three of us were together, the chemistry was hot, much better than any coupled sex that I ever had. Our typical sexual repertoire was this . . . they would tie me up and blindfold me, and then lubricate me from head to toe with lotion.

My penis was always the center of attention. I would either be in her or be in my friend, the latter being a bit more tight. Because I couldn't see anything, all the sensations I felt were even more exaggerated. We used vibrators, clitoral stimulators, ropes, cuffs, lotions, dildos . . . she would sit on top of me with her rear to my face, and at the same time, she would be down on my best friend.

She would come and sit on my face while my friend would sit on my penis and let me penetrate his anus. The variations were endless and so were our orgasms.

Taking a Swing

"Wayne" works in an office supply store in Harrisburg, Pennsylvania. He is thirty-five years old and divorced.

I answered Betty and Max's ad in a magazine several years ago. They said they were looking for men for threesomes. I got a call from Max a couple of weeks after I wrote them. After talking for a while we set up a meeting at Denny's for the following evening. They said they never swing on the first meeting so not to expect anything. They were a very nice couple about my age. Betty wore a loose-fitting raincoat the whole time so I really couldn't tell anything about her shape. She was about five feet five inches tall, brown hair and eyes, and it appeared that she was fairly thin. We talked about lots of different things for about an hour, getting along real well. I then excused myself to go to the men's room. When I got back they asked if I was interested in swinging and if I was always willing to use a condom. I agreed and they said they would get back to me.

The next morning I got a call from them asking if I would like to come over that afternoon. I agreed quickly, as I was very horny.

When I got there Betty was wearing a baggy sweatshirt and jeans. She clearly had a nice ass and I could see the outline of some very good boobs. She said Max would be right back. We had a beer and talked about kids for a while (Max was taking theirs to a friend's house). When Max came back, Betty suggested we get in the Jacuzzi and I quickly agreed.

When I saw Betty I was not disappointed. She had nice, firm breasts, a flat stomach and really fine legs. We got in and Max told me that Betty likes to start by having both of us kiss her neck, nibble on her ears and stroke her thighs. Max and I got right to work. We took turns playing with her pussy with our fingers while our mouths worked on her neck and ears. Max kissed her mouth very passionately and I couldn't resist sucking on a nipple as she lifted herself out of the water high enough for me to get at it without drowning. My fingers found her clit and I gently rubbed it. Betty's hands found my cock and began to stroke it. I was really hot and worrying that I might shoot my load in the Jacuzzi. Max's fingers replaced mine in Betty's hole as I moved up to her other breast. Betty was very turned on by now. Her nipples were very large and hard. She told us we had better get inside.

We quickly got out and dried off more or less and went into their bedroom. Max told me he likes to start off watching, and Betty got on the bed, spread her legs wide and told me to climb on. Her pussy was wet and she started to rub her clit. She had gorgeous, large brown pussy lips that cried out for me to suck them. I really wanted to eat her first because her pussy was sooo nice, but Betty said, "I want you to stroke me, Wayne, with that nice cock of yours." Max gave me a condom and I quickly put it on. My cock was rock hard as I eased it into Betty's wet hole. It felt so good as I made shallow penetrations into her. Max was sitting next to us with quite a hard-on of his own, which he was slowly stroking. The tip was getting wet with his precome. "doesn't she feel wonderful, Wayne?" he asked. I told him she was nice and tight and slippery, all ready for a good fucking. "No, give it to me hard and long, Wayne," she told me. I started fucking her deeper and harder. Betty's legs were wide apart, opening herself to me. "Oh, stroke me, Wayne, stroke it," she said.

I was on my elbows watching her beautiful tits move back and forth as I rammed my cock in her. Her nipples were stiff and got even stiffer as Max's hand came over to squeeze them. I got up into a kneeling position to give Max room to suck Betty's breasts. Betty started to come, squeezing my cock while saying "stroke it, stroke it." I couldn't hold back and started to shoot my load deep into Betty. Betty grabbed Max's cock and jacked him off, stopping just about when it seemed he would start to come.

We stopped to rest for a while and then Max offered Betty his cock to suck. She got him nice and hard by alternating licking his cockhead and sucking it while squeezing his balls. She then turned on her side, lifting one leg up, and Max slipped his cock in from behind. I was still limp from my first orgasm, but this scene was definitely attracting my interest. Betty asked me if I would lick her clit while Max fucked her. I had never done that before, but the idea felt good—my cock reacted instantly—so I got my face down between her legs. I watched as Max's cock slowly went in and out of Betty's pussy. She was so wet that every time he pulled his cock out more juices flowed out. It was getting me very aroused and I felt my cock begin to harden. I lay down next to Betty. I started licking her clit while I watched (at least with one eye) Max's big cock plunge in and out. I was pretty excited but it got even better as Betty began to suck my cock. I heard Max tell Betty he loved watching her blow me. I could hardly concentrate on licking her stiff clit, but I guess I did a good enough job because Betty started to come. As she came, I pressed my tongue hard against her clit and moved it just a slight bit. Her sucking got more intense

and I started to feel the come in my balls getting ready to explode. When I saw Max's cock start to twitch and his come
started oozing out of Betty's cunt, I lost it. My cock started
jerking and load after load shot out into Betty's waiting
mouth. Betty was getting too sensitive, so I stopped eating
her and Max eased his cock out of her. We lay there a long
time resting and then got back into the Jacuzzi. We started
up again, but unfortunately it was getting time for them to
pick up their kids so we had to stop.

It was really a turn-on to be so close to Betty's pussy as she
was being fucked. On subsequent occasions I was the one
fucking while Max licked her clit.

Night on the Town

"Hank," fifty years old, is a real-estate broker in Las Vegas, Nevada.
He has written up this fantasy as a story with an all-purpose "you" as
the woman.

Tonight will be a night you will not forget for a long time.
A very close friend and I are going to take you out to dinner,
to a porno movie and then home, where you will be fucked
like you have never been fucked before. Prepare yourself for
an evening of sex with sucking and fucking in as many
places as you have openings, not to mention eating and
sucking cock until you are as full of come as you would ever
want to be.

We pick you up and you are wearing a silk dress, which
clings to your body, revealing firm breasts with nipples so
hard they show through the fabric to everyone, proclaiming,
"This woman is going to be fucked tonight."

As we drive to the restaurant I put you between us and

begin to run my hands around your nipples until they are as hard as little cocks. Reaching inside the dress, I massage each nipple and you go for my cock. Unzipping my pants, you reach inside and wrap your hand around a shaft that is so hard it feels like it might burst. While my left hand is playing with your tits, my right hand slides up your leg until I'm high enough to realize that you are not wearing panties. I run my finger up and down an already dripping pussy.

I am ready to start the evening right on the spot and begin to finger-fuck you while you respond with little moans that tell me you are ready to come for the first of many times. You shiver as you come and kiss me with your warm, wet mouth, sliding your tongue inside to explore as we both try to suck each other off.

You realize that my cock needs some relief and you put your ass closer to Jim so that you can bend over and give me head while he continues to drive. Your mouth covers my cock with hot, wet lips and you begin to run your tongue around the head, sucking the precome and licking the shaft, which is swollen but pulsating with the movement of your mouth up and down. I pull your head totally down on me so that my cock hits the back of your throat, which seems to make you suck harder. In a few minutes, I am ready to give you an appetizer for the evening—enough come to choke you if you were not already experienced at having my cock deep within your throat. I shoot my load and you swallow and swallow because you have never had so much come in one load in your life.

I can sense that Jim wants some head, too. You turn your body toward him with your ass facing me, unzip him and remove his cock carefully, licking as you begin to take his prick into your mouth. While you are busy blowing him, I have begun to play with your ass and to finger-fuck you from the rear . . . dipping my finger into your pussy juices and sliding my fingers in your come. I spread your love juices up around your ass as I begin to slide one finger in your ass and one in your cunt. You squeal as much as you can with Jim's cock in your mouth, and I know then that when we get home tonight you will enjoy having one cock in your pussy and another in your ass at the same time. This may be a new experience for you, and if so, it will be one you will always cherish. We are only a block away from the restaurant and Jim lets you have his first full load for the evening. Neither of us is accustomed to sharing our ladies with the other, but since we are such good friends and we both know you want to be fucked by two men at the same time, we have agreed.

Dinner is uneventful except for the fact that during the whole time our hands have been playing with each other. At one point, I have slipped off my shoe and put my toe just inside your dripping pussy where I can feel you grip it with your well-toned lips and come while I move around the slipperiness. You have been playing with both our cocks, first Jim's and then mine, and you know the best part of the evening is still ahead.

As we leave the restaurant, I grab you by the ass and squeeze. My hand slips between your legs and I massage your cunt from behind, knowing full well that with Jim walking behind no one will see what I am doing. We are now ready for the second part of the evening. This time I drive, since Jim wants you to lick and suck his prick. We've agreed to share and share alike. What I get, he gets. It's his turn and I don't mind taking the wheel. I pull into the parking lot beside the movie theater and wait while you two finish. The sign out front shows that we will be seeing a triple-X-rated gang bang feature with three men and three women.

The three of us hold hands as we go inside. As we watch the movie, we are kissing you and playing with your pussy. The silk dress has buttons down the front and I unfasten them one by one and drop to my knees in front of you, spreading your legs wide so that I can get my tongue deep into your hot pussy. Everyone else in the theater is also sucking and fucking. Your pussy is shaved the way I like it. I run my tongue along the lips, stopping at the clit and massaging it until you come again and again. Jim takes my place between your legs and while he has his way with your pussy, I nibble your tits and hold my hand over your mouth to stifle your moans of pleasure. We have all but forgotten about the movie, which is a standard fuck-and-suck epic. But who needs it when you can do your own fucking and sucking?

The movie ends but the management knows enough not to turn up the lights or they will see couples going at it all over the place. Doggy-style with the woman leaning forward over the back of the seat seems to be the favorite position.

We leave. On the way home we stop to buy some champagne, which Jim and I will drink out of your pussy. The drive is subdued. We're temporarily satisfied and just play. You jerk us off simultaneously, a cock in each hand, stroking slowly . . . knowing full well that the totally uninhibited screwing is going to continue throughout the night.

From all outward appearances the three of us seem to be on our best behavior as we walk from the car into the house. Immediately after the door is closed we take off our clothes as quickly as possible and run for the hot tub. It is warm and refreshing as our bodies slide deeply into the water. There is some horseplay at first, but we are not here for that. As Jim begins to kiss you I have my hands on your tits, pulling them together, sucking each in turn and kneading them with my fingers. I move back and forth, from one to the other, at times biting gently as your nipples get hard, sending a sensuous shock through you. The fondling has brought you to another climax. I feel you quiver, my hand reaches for your pussy and again, even underwater, you are so slick with your own come that it is no trouble to fuck you with my hand, which slides in and out of the very slick cunt.

I raise you out of the tub and put you on the side while Jim jumps out and gets ready for you to suck him off. You are perched on the edge, legs spread wide. I'm behind, massaging your back as you gobble Jim's cock. His eyes are closed and his mouth is open. I move around between the two of you and get down on my knees so that I can eat you as you suck him. Some of Jim's come drips down on me as he fires away and the excess leaks from your lips. He backs away and I stand up, spin you around and begin to fuck you from behind. I begin to pump slowly at first and when I feel your muscles tighten around my shaft the pleasure is almost unbearable and we both come together.

The bottle of champagne is opened, glasses poured for each of us and we relax on floor cushions, our bodies intertwined. Jim splashes some of the champagne on your pussy and licks it off. This starts things going again—the main event! I lie on my back, you straddle me and take my cock into your pussy. Then Jim comes around behind you and pushes you forward onto your knees. He inserts his prick into your ass and slowly, carefully buries it to the hilt. The three of us, interconnected now, rock back and forth. We've come so often that the moment is prolonged. You grip my cock with your pussy muscles and his with your anal muscles. You moan and ask for more. We both thrust harder and harder, the momentum building. Unplanned, without holding back, the three of us explode together. There are moans of ecstasy the like of which we've never uttered or heard before.

We lie there in this sandwich position savoring the moment, your muscles still holding our cocks. We drift together into a sort of twilight zone, knowing that the night is still young.

Celebrity Watching

"Adam" lives in Charlotte, North Carolina. He's forty-two years old, a furniture salesman, and tells us, "I've been married for eleven years and have four beautiful children.

My number-one fantasy is a ménage à trois, but not the usual threesome that everyone dreams about. Most men want a ménage à trois with two other women. My fantasy is a bit different. It involves my wife, Jean Claude Van Damme and myself.

Now you are probably asking, why Jean Claude? My wife and I find him to be the model of complete and absolute masculinity, and I prefer to have another man in our mix because it removes a lot of my performance pressure.

Anyway, my night would shape out to be something like this: My wife and Jean Claude are on the bed and I'm watching them. He moves down on my wife and starts to eat her out. I see his tongue going inside her and flickering the lips of her vagina. I start to get aroused from this visual and start rubbing myself over my boxers. I decide to join them. I come behind Jean Claude while he is down on my wife and start to massage his strong shoulders and tight ass. I am giving him a total body rubdown as he is pleasing my wife. I feel his sculpted muscles and want to put myself inside of him. I slide my penis into him from the rear and my thrusts are pushing his face into my wife's vagina, deeper and deeper. I pull his hips toward me and start to bang my balls against his ass. My wife's moaning and my strong impact make me come all over him.

I pull out and while he is licking her sex, I go on top of her and put her breasts in my mouth, focusing on her nipples . . . teasing them, sucking them, making them extremely hard. After she comes, she lies down on the bed and proceeds to move down onto him. She puts his penis in her mouth and slides her lips up and down the shaft.

I lie on the bed beside them, masturbating. The deeper she takes him into her mouth the harder and faster I stroke myself. Finally, I climb on top of her from behind and put myself in. I can still see Jean Claude's prick sliding in and out of my wife's mouth and I'm driving myself into her, trying to control my hard-on. Not easy!

After he comes, I pull out and arrange my wife on the bed, stretched on her back with her legs spread. We take turns putting ourselves into her. When I'm in and he's watching, I jerk him off. When he's in and I'm watching, he jerks me off. The three of us finally lie side by side. I'm in the middle. Jean Claude puts his penis inside me and I put mine into my wife, and the three of us start grinding and humping one another. Each of us is holding the person in front extremely tightly against our bodies while we penetrate. Suddenly, a tidal wave overcomes us, as we shake in orgasm for the millionth time it seems.

The Masquerade

"Tim" is forty years old. He lives in Milwaukee where he is an advertising copywriter. He tells us that he created this fantasy to entertain his wife, Anna. There's an additional man in this fantasy but the theme is unchanged.

A warm night in Hawaii, in a condo bedroom above crashing waves, Anna is lying on her bed, languorously, in a diaphanous gown. Window curtains are swaying in the warm gentle wind. Through the right window a man appears wearing a yellow mask and nothing else, through the left window a man appears wearing a red mask and nothing else. Then the door opens and standing there are two more guys, one in a black mask and the other in blue. All of them gather around Anna's bed. The red mask opens Anna's legs and slides between them with his tongue out. Anna wakes up, rubs her eyes and says, "I'd love a good fuck from all you strong, muscular guys." Then she removes her nightgown so that she is butt naked.

Red opens her pussy lips like the petals of a flower, then sticks his tongue on her clit and massages it. Up and down and round and round. Meanwhile, Yellow puts his lips on her left nipple and massages that. Blue puts his lips on her right nipple and massages. Anna sighs, moves her hands forward and grabs the dicks of the blue and yellow guys and plays with them gently. Black puts his lips on Anna's lips, their tongues meeting and meshing against each other.

Red has made a mushy cocktail of cunt-juice and mouth-juice in Anna's cunt, and her clit and pussy lips are now all hot and wet. Anna says, "Fuck me, please. Fuck me." Red slides his cock inside Anna's cunt, Black slides his cock inside Anna's mouth and Yellow and Blue stroke her armpits. Yellow's hand moves down her side, across her thigh and he plays with her pubic hair. Blue follows the same route on her other side and goes for Anna's clit, diddling and teasing it, sometimes in rhythm, sometimes out of rhythm. Sea waves keep crashing below . . . mingling with the sounds of fucking. The curtains sway in the warm gentle wind.

Anna is now hot. She pushes Red down, sliding her cunt down his cock. Yellow is squeezing her boobs and licking a nipple. Blue is licking the other nipple and diddling her clit. Anna's long auburn hair is touching the shoulders of the two guys. Red grabs Anna's butt tightly. Black slides between the mass of people and sticks his cucumber-sized hard cock inside Anna's mouth. Fuck, fuck, fuck, fuck, fuck, fuck. The fucking continues. Anna comes. She keeps fucking and comes again. She smiles and says, "Okay, folks, everybody rotates."

The group pauses. There's a break for drinks and sandwiches. Then back to work. Yellow gets the cunt this time, Blue gets her mouth, Black gets the right boob and the clit, while Red takes the boob and crotch-hair. They fuck and then they rotate again until everyone has had the cunt . . . then they take another pause, more drinks and snacks and dreams of the next fuck play.

Anna says she wants to go out onto the darkened beach and do it doggy-style. They all saunter out, lie under the palm trees with moonlight on them. Red puts his very substantial cock into a very juicy cunt, Yellow grabs a boob and crotch-hair, and Blue takes her other boob, and as he softly diddles her clit, slides behind her and penetrates her ass. Black isn't left out. He comes around to the front and inserts his cock in Anna's mouth. Balls slam into Anna's butt. She says, "I love it. Fuck me more." Cocks slide in and out. Red comes with a roar, then Black comes in Anna's mouth. Blue lets go into her ass. There's a break to give Yellow his chance at Anna's cunt. Then they all sit in the sand, have another drink and plan the next fuck.

One of the themes in these fantasies that may not be obvious at first is the strong desire to arouse the woman and supply her with pleasure. Of course, the men are enjoying themselves and each other, too. But the fantasies create a "provider" role for the men that is in keeping with this defining male characteristic.

I know it bothers some women to be told that men see themselves as "breadwinners." They assume that this implies that they—women—need their bread won for them. Big men, little women is not the issue, as far as I'm concerned. This provider role is far from being self-assigned. It comes either with the genes or with several thousand years of cultural conditioning. Maybe both. Men aren't going to be "rewired" anytime soon.

As providers of sexual satisfaction—being good lovers—men are in a more ambiguous area than they are as providers of physical sustenance. The hunter knows when he is a good hunter. He kills a bear and skins it. The lover isn't so sure of his competence, however. The desire to arouse the women that we see in this chapter's fantasies is so strong that to do the "job" he brings in reinforcements.

In general, the group-sex fantasy challenges the notion of "woman as chattel," or property. These women are not beholden to one man for sexual satisfaction, and in the fantasies, at least, the men recognize, accept and sometimes promote this arrangement.

As with all taboo breaking, there are subversive acts involved. A ménage à trois amounts to embracing a new math of sexuality. The men and women are cut loose from the couple as the one and only equation. I've been told by those who have acted out this fantasy that it is both liberating and frightening. They say there is a sense of discovery, new possibilities and innovation. But the downside is that the old comfort zone no longer exists. There's a whole new dynamic at work and it takes a lot of getting used to. A sexual relationship between two people is complicated in its own right. As the numbers increase so does the complexity.

Fantasy allows the fantasizer to "run the numbers" and check out the bottom line without having to live with the consequences. In general, this remains one of the leading attractions of fantasies no matter what the theme.

Eight

Secret Numbers:
Group Sex

I have a suspicion that the orgy fantasy loses some of its appeal over time. I can't prove it because my sample is too small, but the men in this chapter tend to be younger. The oldest is thirty-three and the others are clustered around their late teens and twenties.

It stands to reason that at the hormonal high-water mark, men would imagine themselves ready, willing and able to make it during any given lunch hour with a randomly selected multitude of the world's most desirable actresses, models and *Baywatch* wannabes.

Ah, to be young, randy and mildly delusional!

The fantasy in that case is an excellent way to boil off excess sexual energy. In between actual real-life sexual encounters—whether few and far between or frequent and frenzied—he can amuse himself with fantasy visits to the sultan's harem. But as men acquire age and experience, the idea of an orgy, while still appealing, is tempered by practical considerations and self-knowledge—like, "one good woman is plenty, thanks."

But while they last, group sex fantasies—in multiples of more than three—are entertaining, and probably, entertainment is their primary function.

Group sex is one fantasy that is inherently difficult to act out. The logistical hurdles are daunting, and so is the risk of rejection and ridicule. It's much easier and safer to remain in the realm of fantasy. Asking your date if you can stay the night is hard enough, let alone arranging for eight women and a trampoline.

Inside that safe haven of fantasy, men are allowed to practice a lavish and unrestrained sexuality the likes of which is hardly ever attainable in real life. This exuberance and limitlessness is a large measure of the appeal. These are not dark fantasies, by any means. There is a joyousness and a freshness to them. Both the men and the women throw themselves totally into the experience. There's no holding back, no reticence or asexuality on either side.

A group-sex fantasy offers men a visual feast. I think it explains the attractiveness, in large part, to the entire genre from the ménage à trois to the ménage à fifty. There is much to see and much to become aroused by.

And little to fear. There is a sense of shared responsibility within the group that dilutes and dissipates guilt. Taboos are being broken right and left but everybody's doing it—literally.

There are no guilty bystanders, and no innocent bystanders, either.

Motel Six

"Peter" is twenty. He works in a marina near New London, Connecticut. A sailing enthusiast, he dropped out of college after two years to be near the water. "Peter" says he will probably finish his degree "one of these days."

Think of his fantasy as a ménage à trois times two.

I guess that all men dream about having several women at the same time, but my dream goes beyond that. I fantasize about having the maximum number of women at one time that I can. I know that I won't be able to satisfy each of them sexually, but as it's my fantasy it really doesn't matter. I don't have a lot of sexual experience and have never received or given oral sex. I've never even fully explored a woman's pubic region so my fascination with looking at and touching pussies is reflected in my fantasy.

Here goes: I'm lying on my back in bed. I'm totally naked. My legs are spread wide apart and my arms are stretched out above my head. A bevy of six beautiful women walk into the room. They're all slim and naked. My cock, which has already started to stiffen, becomes totally erect as they stand around the bed. They start to rub themselves, running their fingers up and down their pussy lips, spreading them so that I can see their innermost secrets. I stare at each one of them in turn, comparing the different shapes and sizes of their vulvas.

The first woman crawls onto the bed and straddles my stomach. First, she opens her mouth and slowly takes my cock inside her and sucks it for a while. Then she uses her fingers to spread wide her pussy lips so that I can see her clit sticking out. With the other hand, she holds my cock and guides it into her pussy, moving her body slowly up and down so that my cock slides deep into her. All this time she is holding her pussy lips apart.

After a while, she raises her body and my cock falls out of her and she moves toward my face and lowers her pussy onto my mouth. She is still holding apart her lips and I suck her protruding clit. As I am sucking her, I place a finger inside her and rub the wet, hot inner walls of her body.

Shortly, she moves away from me and sits on the edge of the bed. Then the next woman does exactly the same thing, but this time there is one difference. When she sucks my cock, it is covered with the love juices of the previous woman, and that excites me greatly.

After each woman has done the same to me, I have already penetrated each of them with my cock and my fingers and have sucked on their clits and had a chance to examine them close up. Now, as I feel myself close to orgasm, the women organize themselves for my ultimate fantasy. My legs and arms are once again spread wide and the first woman sits astride one of my feet. She holds my foot and rubs my toes into her pussy and although they don't go in very far, I can feel the warmth of her as I penetrate her body. The second woman does the same with the other foot.

A third woman sits astride one of my hands and I insert a finger into her love hole. As she gets hotter and wetter, I find that I am able to put three fingers inside her. The fourth woman does the same with my other hand and soon I am pinned to the bed by four beautiful women.

The fifth woman again straddles my body and lowers herself onto my cock, now almost bursting with excitement. I watch it as it disappears inside her body until all I can see is her swollen clit between her wide spread pussy lips. The final woman kneels over my head and I can see her pussy in all its glory.

I had picked this one especially for the climax of my fantasy because she had the sweetest taste of all the women. The constant rubbing of her pussy lips has made her pubic hair wet with love juices and I can clearly see every detail of her vulva and clitoris. I open my mouth and start to lick along the gateway to her sex. As I do so, I feel the bed rocking as each of the women bounces up and down and my fingers and toes become wetter and hotter as nectar flows out of their bodies.

The woman holding my cock within her is also bouncing up and down and I feel the tip of my rod thrusting against the end walls of her pussy.

As my passion increases, I open my mouth and suck as much of the clit and vulva into my mouth as I can. All of the women are rubbing and pulling their own clits except for the one whose pussy is in my mouth. Instead she is pulling and squeezing her nipples. Although it is hard for me to concentrate, my fingers still thrust deep into the bodies of the women who are on my hands while the women on my feet are using my toes to bring themselves to climax. I can feel the shuddering of the woman's pussy that I'm sucking on and I have to swallow harder to take in all the fluid she is producing.

I feel myself explode, shooting my juices into the woman who is riding my cock, and she keeps moving up and down until the last drops are squeezed from me. I feel her lift her body off mine and then her lips are on my cock, licking up the mixture of my semen and her own juices that covers me. One by one, the other women leave the places on my body and take it in turns to lick my cock until it is clean.

The woman who had received my orgasm in her pussy lies down on the bed with her legs wide apart. I lie beside her with my face almost touching her pussy. One by one the other women take turns cleaning my semen from within her cunt. They stick one finger into her and then lick it clean. Then they spread her pussy lips and lick along her vulva, teasing her slit, now red and hot. All this time, I just stare at the woman's pussy as it is cleaned by the other women, fondling breasts and pussies as they take turns to lick her. This constant touching and watching soon makes me hard again . . . but that's another fantasy.

In Harem's Way

"Benton" is a thirty-three-year-old civil engineer, living in Morgan City, Louisiana. He says, "I've been in a relationship for four or five months but it's not that serious. But then again, who knows?"

My fantasy involves a harem of women of all sorts. There would be a bunch of different outfits, and they'd take on the role of their apparel. One would be a "Barbie" type, another in leather, a third an "Uncle Sam" type doing it "for her country," a fourth would be an "I Dream of Jeannie" type, a fifth would be a slutty porn queen and . . . let's go with those for now.

They would start by fanning me and feeding me grapes. While two of them concentrated on my comfort, the other three would concentrate on my pleasure by kissing, sucking and licking every digit of my body. The one in leather would be particularly aggressive, sucking on my cock and gripping me while I move in and out of her. So while she is licking my sex, the porn queen would be fingering my asshole and rubbing her wet vagina against me.

My Jeannie would take turns kissing me and shoving her tongue down my throat. The patriotic one would be fanning me while she fingers Jeannie. It would be a big fucking orgy, where everything goes and everyone gets satisfied—mainly me.

Anyway, as my hard-on grows in the leather-clad girl's mouth, she stops and starts to suck on my balls. Just when

I'm about to burst from the pleasure, they all stop what they are doing and turn around with their legs open so wide that I can see their hard clits dangling. I have all these beautiful women who want to feel me inside them and I take time injecting them with my beef. Of course, I am like a machine, so I don't come instantly. I keep ripping into their flesh with the uttermost force that is humanly possible while I grip their breasts, and stimulate their clits at the same time.

While I'm pleasing one, they finger each other and suck on whatever breast is available while they wait their turn. But I am the star, and they all want me. When I finally come, I share my juices with all of them and inject myself spurt by spurt into their flesh. I collapse onto the ground, and they all surround me, continuing to pamper me with all of their affection and the pleasure of their bodies. I can feel their bodies grinding against mine, kissing me from head to toe, and doing everything in their power to tease and please me.

"Benton's" real-life sexual experience parallels the fantasy.

I went to this S&M club with two girls whom I had just recently met. This place was a sight like I had never seen. Guys dressed as girls, girls dressed as guys, people being whipped against a wall, chained dominatrix's subjects . . . I think you get the picture.

Let's just say this was a tremendous visual explosion and I didn't know where to look. Thank goodness for peripheral vision!

Anyway, the three of us are watching the show go on, and I think, needless to say, we are getting aroused by it all. Suddenly, I look across the table and one of the girls has disappeared. Then, under the table, I feel my legs being pushed open. I look down and she is sticking her hands up my pant legs and caressing my calves. The other woman moves beside me and begins to kiss and lick my neck. As I start to tongue her in response, I feel a draft below my belt. My fly is open and the one under the table is stroking my penis like a madwoman. The harder she strokes me the deeper I shove my tongue down the other's throat. I take my hand and slide it down into her shirt and fondle her breasts. I can feel a tongue going up and down the length of my penis. Between this licking of my sex, and the foreplay up top, and the visual delight around me, my hard-on must be reaming out her throat due to the nearly explosive engorgement that's occurring.

The one sitting next to me slides her hand down the back of my pants and sticks her finger in my asshole. I start to move up and down so that her finger stings me like a sharp knife. At the same time, my penis is bouncing up and down in the other's mouth. I take my face and smother it in the breasts to my right, sucking and licking almost in a frenzy. Below, my penis is being devoured and I can feel my juices ready to explode. I want to fuck the shit out of both of them, but we were trying to remain as discreet as possible, and so far we hadn't been noticed yet.

In the meantime, across the room, this one girl is getting whipped and I could hear her scream—which was making me crazy! She's in a squat position, and the whip is running between her legs, stinging her crotch and anal canal. The more she gets whipped, the more blood rushes into my cock until I can't take it anymore. I come pouring into her mouth and she swallows every last drop of juice that I have given her. The other one beside me takes her finger out of my asshole and puts it in her mouth . . . moving her finger in and out, tasting me. The three of us reconvene around the table, enjoying the sights of the club, and then go back to my place to continue the festivities.

Winter Wonderland

"Terry" is twenty-four years old. He's a buyer for a jewelry manufacturer and lives in Providence, Rhode Island.

My fantasy definitely involves more than one woman—three, to be precise. They are all model material, about six feet tall, large breasts, between 125 and 130 pounds, with super long, tan legs. One's a blonde, the second is a brunette and the third is a redhead.

We are in a rustic cabin in the woods, a very secluded place, and it is the middle of winter. There's a fire going in the living room and the three bombshells are all wearing very sexy lingerie: white lace with satin trim around the breasts and crotch area. The three women are lying on the bearskin rug, and I am stretched out naked on the couch watching them.

They start to play around by sucking on each other's breasts and sticking their fingers between the crevices of the form-fitting satin. I lie on the couch stroking myself, while the brunette sticks her tongue inside the crotch of the blonde. The redhead takes the brunette's breasts and begins to mold them in her hands. The moaning and the licking and the sucking is making me stroke my hard-on faster and faster until I feel the need to join in and fuck someone.

I put on a condom and pull the blonde up to the couch and mount her. In an instant, I'm pounding my dick inside of her. As I fuck her with all the energy I have, the redhead lowers herself onto the blonde's face and begins to spread the lips of her vagina all over her mouth. While the blonde is being fucked she is also eating out the pussy of the redhead and enjoying every minute of it. While the redhead is being eaten out, she pulls the brunette next to her and shoves her face in between her breasts and begins to lick and suck them, paying particular attention to the nipple area. The brunette is getting so aroused by having her tits sucked that she jabs her finger inside herself and starts to scream at the top of her lungs in pleasure.

All this sexual energy is really getting me going, so I take the blonde and flip her over onto all fours and lay it into her real good. My balls are slapping against her ass, and the others are giving me a complete body rubdown.

Just as the blonde begins to moan, on the verge of orgasm, I slide my hand around and begin to stimulate her clit with precise steadiness and speed. Two seconds later, she comes all over the place, and I throw her aside and reach for the next one. The blonde retires and goes to sit on the couch and watches the action. I grab the redhead and slide her underneath me. I start to pound away at her, and she throws her arms around my waist and flips me over. She's on top of me and begins to rock me back and forth, while the brunette takes a seat on my face. The juices of the brunette are running down my face and they are as sweet as honey. I can't wait to be inside of her so I put all my efforts into making the redhead come. I grab her by the hips and steadily push her back and forth onto my bulging hard-on until she can't take any more and lets out little contractions with spurts of her fluid. I throw her off me and eye the prize that I have been waiting for—the one who is going to make me come all over the place.

The redhead takes a seat next to the blonde and they begin making out. The brunette lowers herself onto my body and takes my balls into her mouth while she looks at me innocently. My hard-on is poking her in the face, and I can't wait to get inside of her. I turn her round and send my cock up her butt. I am shoving my penis up her anal canal, a sensation that so far beats everything else.

I wrap my arms around her waist and she jerks her body up against mine, taking her breasts into her hands and stimulating her nipples. At the point of impact with her anus, she gasps and her juices dribble down her legs and all over the bearskin rug. I pull out and put myself inside her until I come all over the place and we collapse into each other's arms . . . we join the others on the couch to watch the fire crackle and engage in some heavy petting.

Truck Start

"Stewart" is nineteen years old. A student, he lives in Vermont. He says he is a virgin and "not proud of the fact."

There are three women. All of them are slim and beautiful. The first one wears nothing but silk, the second is dressed in leather from head to foot and the third goes in for plastic clothes in weird colors—either that or in some variations of the fantasy she is naked (except for boots).

They are truck drivers. They own their own trailer rig. It's painted pink and white with a big sign that says "The Love and Sex People, Inc." I'm standing there admiring the sign when the leather lady approaches and asks, "Would you like to see what's inside?" I say okay and she opens the back for me to get in. The next thing I know she is prodding me with a whip toward a huge rotating wheel that is set up like a wheel of fortune. She starts beating me with the whip and I pass out. When I come to, I'm tied to the wheel with leather straps. The three women are taking turns spinning the wheel and whipping me. I scream and the woman in the silk removes her panties and gags me with them. The lovely smell gives me an orgasm.

After I come, I doze off and when I awake I'm in a huge bed. It's the size of two king-size beds together. There are satin sheets and mink-covered pillows. I'm tied down with leather straps, pantyhose, and silk scarves.

The next thing they do is pour Crisco oil all over my body. Did I mention that I'm naked? They tease me by rubbing the oil around my body and licking it with their tongues. Just when that starts to turn me on they stop. Eventually, the three ladies untie me and carefully clean off the oil. They're very gentle. Then they tie me up again and each one takes a turn having her way with me.

Oral sex first, and then the big one—home run—and I'm no longer a virgin. Miss Leather does the honors and then silk and plastic have a go. Between the whipping and the sex with three women I'm hurting.

The three want to give me a reminder of the experience. Miss Leather straps me into a chastity belt made of heavy steer hide. Silk fits me out with a pair of panties that she slips on over the chastity belt. Plastic does me up in a see-through vinyl straitjacket. Then they take me to the hospital.

In the last chapter I referred to the new math of sexuality. Well, here, the old math is involved, too. Namely, multiplication.

In a group-sex fantasy, the fantasizer is getting more of everything that really turns him on. The multiplier effect is working overtime. If he has a breast fetish, there's two, four, six, eight, ten breasts to work with. Less is not more in a group or ménage à trois—more is more!

This abundance comes through loud and clear, but I think there is another important element in the group fantasy that gets lost in the retelling, or at least diluted. We are on the outside looking in at these stories and, as a result, there is a certain distance. All the characters seem equal. Yet, the creator is at ground zero. He is more equal. The powerful appeal of a fantasy comes from the focus it throws onto the fantasizer. He—or she in the case of female fantasies—is usually the center of attention throughout the action. After all, the fantasizer is the narrator of the story, filtering the events through his unique consciousness. He is both the eye and "I" of the story. What he says goes.

This is not only a control issue. Being at the center of attention enhances a person's sense of desirability. It is rewarding and indispensable when it occurs in a traditional one-on-one sexual relationship. Both partners need to know they are desired, and an elaborate choreography takes place—or should be taking place—to insure that it is the case. Unsatisfactory sex is often one-sided, selfish sex that deprives one of the partners of this essential feeling of being wanted by the other. But sometimes, through no one's fault, it just happens.

However, it never happens in a fantasy. The scriptwriter sees to that. In a group, the fantasizer has ratcheted up his desirability by a factor equal to the number of other partners that he is involved with. The blonde is nuts for him and so are the redhead and the brunette, the biker and the lady doctor.

Finally, the group-sex fantasy is an act of communal taboo breaking. He is not alone, but acting in consort with others who share the same feelings and sexual longings. He is being bad—and that's always exhilarating—but not so bad that he is in danger of becoming an outcast. Taboos hold such a powerful influence that the solitary iconoclast can end up feeling that he or she has gone too far. The group acts as a counterweight to the marginalizing forces. There is safety in numbers.

I could close the chapter at this point, but before I do I want go back to a point I made earlier about the multiplier effect. The group multiplies validation and, above all, I think this is what keeps men coming back to the group-sex fantasy even as they age and begin to realize that quality may be preferable to quantity. Validation, however, can be in such short supply in many traditional relationships, for whatever reason, that this exercise in the new math adds up to pleasure and satisfaction.

Nine

Secrets Exposed: Sex in Public

The bedroom is out. Boring!

Some of the hottest sex takes place in public these days. At least that's what I'm told by men and women who claim to know from first-hand experience.

I'll take their word for it, but the fantasies that men shared with me indicated that it is a popular theme.

Why?

For one thing, it certainly isn't boring. Fantasies, of all types, offer a refuge from routine and predictable sex. Nothing deadens relationships—or palates—as surely as having the same thing, served in the same way at the same time and the same place, week after week. Fantasies help break the monotony.

I think many people fall into the boredom trap unintentionally, and once in it's difficult to get out. We all lead busy and stressful lives. Frequently the choice is between quick, perfunctory sex and no sex at all. The lesser of two evils is still evil. And when it gets chosen again and again, habits form that are hard to break.

It's one reason that I favor sharing sexual fantasies between partners. Handled diplomatically—and that's extremely important—an exchange of fantasies can help liven things up by alerting your lover to possibilities that he or she hadn't considered. Also, it's a way to prime the erotic pump. Both partners have permission to let their imaginations bubble over.

I say sharing fantasies needs diplomacy because a familiar "script"—to you—may be so alien and threatening to your partner that it could have a destructive impact on your relationship. A fantasy that is substantially at odds with the actual content and context of a couple's sex life could be read as a general indictment of a partner's sexual performance. And maybe that's the message you want to convey. If not, it's probably not a bad idea to put a little "spin" on a fantasy the first time it's shared. One way is to present it as something you read about or dreamed one night. In that way you can gauge reaction.

Overall, the sex-in-public theme is appealing because it is risky, dangerous, "bad." Not only does it get the couple out of the bedroom and into the office or schoolroom, the fantasy is reawakening the forbidden quality that sex once had before being sanctioned by marriage, established relationships or accumulated experience.

Think back. If you ever made love or engaged in heavy petting as a young person in the backseat of a car, part of the thrill was the possibility that "someone" might notice what was happening. The danger heightened the sensation. Holding hands, walking arm and arm, stealing kisses when the chaperones at the prom aren't watching are all ways to savor the dangerous quality that sex offers. There's even some of that in traditional wedding celebrations: the "blushing bride, tossing the garter and teasing the couple about the honeymoon. There's a little whiff of open sexuality in the air.

I think the sex-in-public fantasy is on the same wavelength. However, it crackles with danger and is very thrilling, whereas a wedding is a carefully orchestrated ritual. The fantasy seems to suggest that the lovers are so impassioned, so wildly inflamed for each other that they are no longer in control. They want each other right now and right here, no matter that here and now is at thirty-five thousand feet in a commercial airliner flying to Los Angeles.

This is a sexy notion, and even if it remains just a fantasy it can be a major turn-on. I've interviewed couples who incorporate the sex-in-public fantasy as part of their fore-foreplay, discussing what it would be like to make love then and there while riding in the back of a city bus heading home. When they get home, the couple is ready for steamy sex.

Sex in public is, perforce, sex that's different. The message that comes through loud and clear to me is the desire to strip away the refinement and predictability that reduce sex to just another bodily necessity like food and sleep. These fantasies return sex to the status of one of life's great adventures.

The Eye of the Beholder

When he wrote to us, "William" didn't provide any personal information, instead he got right to the point.

> Here is a little fantasy of mine—pretty tame I admit, but fun for masturbation. Mary is an attractive woman; slight, thin, short blonde hair, very flat-chested. We know each other reasonably well and flirt at the office, but have never dated.
>
> So one day before quitting time, I go to her office and ask a work question. While we talk she is seated, bending over her purse, fishing for something. It's a hot summer day, and she has on a loose blouse, no bra, so I have an unobstructed view of her bare chest—the first time I have seen it this way.

I'm intrigued and excited by her breasts. They are not small mounds as I might have expected, but hang like two flattish triangles, maybe three inches long (she's nursed three children). Her breasts jiggle around delightfully as she hunts. At one point she looks up and catches me staring, but then glances back to her purse. Because of the way she looks down her blouse, though, I'm sure she knows I'm peeking, and that makes me all the more excited, and I feel my face flush and my penis harden in my shorts.

Suddenly Mary looks up again, still not concealing her breasts, and says with a smile, "Are you looking at my tits?" I blush and stammer, "Uh, yeah I guess so, I'm very sorry."

She answers, "Oh, I don't care; there's nothing to look at anyway!"

"On the contrary, they're very attractive."

"You think so? she asks, smiling, as she pushes the door closed with her foot.

Now my penis is really trying to force its way out. Mary stands in front of me and begins to unbutton her blouse. "Well, if you really like them, I don't see why you can't have a good look."

As she drops her blouse off her thin arms, I feast my eyes on her sexy breasts. They lie almost flat against her chest, triangular, with the nipples pointing straight down.

"Between being small to begin with, and then the nursing ruining whatever shape I had, I'm surprised anyone finds my breasts worth looking at," she said, sighing. "My ex certainly didn't. He said they looked like tongues!"

"Mary, they are very sexy," I objected.

"Look," she said, holding her right breast in her hand, "there's not much here to play with."

"Not true!" I had enough of words and placed my hand on her chest under her other breast. I slid it up and lifted the

breast. I bent to her and took her whole breast in my mouth.
As I massaged it with my tongue and sucked on it, Mary
moaned.

"Oh, John, that feels so good!" she gasped as she massaged her other breast.

Suddenly Mary pulled back and her breast smacked out
of my mouth. We both laughed. "Why don't you come to
my apartment for dinner?" she asked, while stroking my
thigh next to my hard cock. "Are you free?"

"You bet," I answered, because I was eating alone that
night.

And . . . but that's another fantasy.

Moving Day

"Frank" is thirty-one. He's gay and lives in Ann Arbor, Michigan. He
has a monogamous relationship with another man and tells us that he
has never had sex with a woman.

My sexual fantasies center on people I work with and, in
general, people whom I find attractive and unattainable. By
unattainable, I mean people of different sexual orientations,
or ones who are currently involved in other relationships.

My number-one fantasy involves a coworker named
Janet. She is in her late twenties, extremely bright and sensual. She dresses to kill—power suits, high pumps, the
whole bit. She is truly a woman who knows what she wants
and how to get it. My phone rings. "Hi, it's Janet. Can you
help me transfer some of my things to my new desk? I'll
come and get you!" She arrives at my desk in a skintight,
short black dress that hugs the contours of her body. "Follow me," she says.

She walks in front of me like a model, waving her hips from side to side. I want to grab her. "You get that box, and I'll get this one," she says. Janet bends down to the floor with her legs open so wide that I can see the g-string that she is wearing. She stays in that position waiting for me to do something. Instead of picking up the box, I kneel in front of her and stick my hand up her skirt. My fingers find her crotch and she rides them. With my free hand I caress her breasts. She melts as I touch her. My bulge is getting so large that I need to put it into her.

We are behind her desk in the corner of the office, which is fairly open, but it is late in the day and there aren't that many people around. I stand up to check to see if the coast is clear. It is and I move behind her and drop on my knees again. I pull her skirt up over her hips, slide my pants down and enter from the rear. In an instant my balls are slapping her ass with intense conviction. She's mine now, and I'm drilling it inside her till I can't take it anymore and explode. She turns and takes me into her mouth and savors my juices. After a few more minutes, Janet straightens her skirt and points to the box. "You get that one and I'll get this one."

Cinema Verité

"Russell" is African-American, forty-five years old and, like "Frank," is also gay and in a long-term monogamous relationship. He's a former male model and now the owner of a bridal boutique in Tallahassee, Florida.

One of my former lovers was a Dallas Cowboys' all-star, which is one reason my fantasies tend to feature professional football players.

We're in a movie theater in a big city. My friend is big, a real heavyweight; the complete epitome of masculinity. We move closer to one another. Our row is empty but there are people all around us. I go in front of him, on the floor, and pull his legs down so that my favorite part is in my face. I begin to rub his penis over the fabric of his pants till his hard-on is bulging and I need to touch it.

I unbuckle his belt, unzip the fly and pull his pants down from his hips. I take his penis in my hands and lick its head before plunging it into my mouth. I move my tongue around and stroke him at the same time.

He opens his legs wider and stretches them on top of the seat back in front. His penis is hardening in my mouth. I start to manually massage his penis and testicles, giving special attention to the area under the testicles near the anal canal. I massage the area persistently with my fingers and tongue, as he gets more and more aroused and starts to jerk off his hard-on. I can't stand this sight any longer. I rip off my pants and put my ass down onto his hardness and start to move up and down, as he controls my hips. I touch myself at the same time, and I'm getting duly satisfied. He wraps his arms around me and every time I come down he puts his hands on my thighs and makes the impact even harder. He comes first and a second later so do I. My cream seems to have the trajectory of a missile, soaring toward the lighted screen.

I turn and the people around us are watching intently, nibbling popcorn as if we were the main feature.

Center of Attention

"Avery" is seventy years old, retired and living in Ocala, Florida. He told us, "I've been married to my second wife for three years. Her first husband is deceased and I'm divorced from my first wife. We met at a singles club down here in Florida.

I'm standing in front of a woman's club, wearing silk panties that I swiped out of my wife's dresser. My hand is in my underwear and I'm masturbating. I have a crowd of women watching me as I stroke myself up and down. I picture them all naked, with their breasts smacking me in the face as I rub myself. I can visualize the women touching each other and licking one another in their private parts. This image sends blood rushing to my penis and I stroke myself faster and faster. I remove the panties I am wearing and rub them against my penis, moving it up and down. The softness of the underwear feels like the inside of a woman and I am trying to control myself from coming.

The women continue to please one another and I can hear their moans and cries, which arouses me all the more. I picture several of the women masturbating in front of me, and I am growing increasingly larger. They are putting their fingers inside of themselves and stroking their breasts at the same time. I want them to lick me, but they are only watching. I'd love to put myself inside them, but somehow, for some reason, I can't get any closer to them. I belong to me and they belong to themselves as a collective unit. They can touch one another but that's all. I see two of the women start to hump one another. They are grinding their bodies against one another, squeezing their fingers in between their legs for penetration. Their breasts are smacking up and down hitting one another, as they embrace them and suck them. This sight is enough for me to rub myself all the harder and rush to the outer limits of my orgasm. With a loud bellow, I come all over their faces.

Late Shift

"Brad" lives in Los Angeles. He is thirty years old and works as an entertainment industry publicist.

I'm working late in the office one evening on my computer when this woman I adore walks into my room. Did I tell you she is married? Well, she is. She, in turn, is working late and asks if I could help with her computer because there seems to be a malfunction.

We go to her office and as I'm trying to figure out the bloody thing, she leans over and kisses me. "I can't believe I just did that," she says, very innocently. Then I lean over, unbutton the top button of her blouse, kiss her breast and say, "No, I can't believe I did that."

We start to kiss and our hands explore each other's bodies. She puts her hand up my shirt and runs her fingers through the hair on my chest. Her hands feel so good that my private parts start to ache and call for them. I unbutton the rest of her blouse and stick my hands underneath her bra, cupping her breasts in my hands.

We take the things on her desk, the lot of it—computer, file folders, books—and dump them on the floor in a jumble. I go to draw the curtain to cover the wall of glass that overlooks the main office. "Leave it," she says, smiling.

I throw her down onto the desk and start stripping her from head to toe. I take my finger and puncture a hole through the crotch area of her stockings and stick my tongue inside of her. She raises her body up into my face and pushes herself against me.

I slide her skirt off and eventually her stockings, and begin to probe and finger her vagina. She holds my hand and shows me how much impact she wants by taking me out and slamming me back in, but I really want to fuck her.

I pull my fingers out and move away from the desk. I slide my shirt off and take my pants down. I stand there in my boxers with my hard-on coming through them. I slide the boxers off and the cock bobs right back up. I take it in my hand and stroke it up and down. "Come here and let me do that for you," she says. She moves off the desk, takes my penis in her hand and gently pulls me down onto the floor. As we kiss passionately, she jerks me off. She lowers herself onto my body and starts to lick the tip with circling motions. Finally, with one big move she takes it all into her mouth and works her head up and down briskly. When my penis aches and I'm about to come, I pull her up by the hair and she settles her hips onto mine. With a slight twist of her torso, my cock slides into her. She's on top and I grab her hips to help her ride me. My head is up so that her tits can smack me in the face.

I want more impact. I lift her body off me, throw her onto the desk, legs on the floor, belly down. I stick my penis inside her anal canal, forcing myself deep into her tight ass. I swing my hands around and rub her vagina, while I continue to violate this woman who does not belong to me. Finally, when I am about to reach the brink, I grab her hips and smack in and out of her ass in quick, short motions until my come drenches her and goes oozing down her body and hers bursts and dribbles down her legs.

What a night!

Class Act

"Gil" is forty-two. He lives in Carson City, Nevada, where he is a public-school teacher. He wrote this fantasy originally for his wife, who finds it a real turn-on.

After a night out, we're driving home when we go by the school where I work. I ask if you'd like to see where I perform educational magic every day, and you say, "Sure." It's about midnight and the place is deserted, so I let us in with my key. We go to my office first, and then down the halls. I show you the classroom where I teach Composition I. As we enter I turn on the bright, cold fluorescent lights.

You go to a table at the front of the class and hop up. As I face you from the traditional spot at the front of the room, you cross your legs and smile devilishly. "What can you teach me, professor?" you ask, as your eyes twinkle brightly. I lean down and kiss you lightly on the lips, while I sensuously rub the back of your neck. You grab my tie and pull me close, as you wrap both arms around my neck and press your full breasts to my chest.

"Tell you what," I say. "I'd like to mark the occasion of your visit with a few pictures." With that, I pull a Polaroid camera from my briefcase and begin taking some snapshots. You pose on the table in a variety of ways, smiling sweetly the entire time. "Show me some cleavage," I urge, and you comply, unbuttoning your silk blouse to reveal the tops of your lovely breasts above your black, lacy bra. After a few more shots, I ask for more, you respond and remove your bra completely, holding your breasts, one in each hand. As I furiously snap away, you begin to roll your hardened nipples between your fingers.

We both breathe harder now, and I put down the camera. I go to the table, gently push you back onto its surface, suck each sweet rosebud into my mouth, and give each the attention it deserves. As your breath quickens even more, I shove my hand under your skirt. Since you're only wearing a garter belt and stockings, access to your love mound is easy. I insert my middle finger deep inside you, and gently rub your clit with another. At the same time, I continue my attention to your breasts, which are heaving wildly up and down now. I lean up, find your lips and force my tongue inside your mouth. You accept it willingly, and begin to suck on it quite hard.

Just as I begin to feel you prepare to come, I disengage myself from your lips, and remove my hand from your crotch. I turn you over on the table, onto your hands and knees. I pull your skirt up over your back. Your lovely ass points proudly up into the air. I bend forward, place my nose in your vagina and begin to tongue your clit, which is quivering and quite hard now. My hands reach under you to fondle your nipples, which are like tiny diamonds. After a few moments, I feel your pussy spasm, clamping down on my nose. Your juices trickle down the tops of your thighs as you moan loudly. "That was wonderful," you say. But I'm not finished. I remove my tongue from your clit and begin to encircle your tight little anus. I begin to lick around the outside, just to tease you. As your breath starts to quicken again, I place my middle finger back into your vagina and swirl it around. Then I insert the tip of my tongue into your ass and thrust it gently back and forth. You moan again and start thrusting your hips back and forth to meet mine. You shiver and come again from the manual stimulation of your clit. The sweet, musky smell fills my nose as I plunge my tongue in and out of you. Then I position you at the end of the table, undo my belt and lower my trousers. I place the tip of my rock-hard cock against your bunghole, first lubricating it with your juices. I slowly, slowly press into you. You moan and I ask if I'm hurting you. You say no, so I press harder. I can feel the tight muscles of your anal walls loosen as I enter, then tightly clamp down again. When I'm in only an inch or two, I begin to gently stroke back and forth. One hand reaches under you and plays with your pussy again, alternating between the clit and the canal. The other hand plays with your breast, flicking the nipple ever so slightly.

We both begin to moan now. The incredible tightness of your ass sends shivers up and down my entire body. I've never felt anything like this before—it's like the first time I ever made love. My head is abuzz with all sorts of sensations. I feel like I might faint. Just then, you reach around with one hand and begin squeezing my balls. This is too much! With a loud yell, I come quickly and violently. My knees shake and almost buckle. Somehow I stay on my feet. My cock begins to go down and slides involuntarily down your crack. You jump as it accidentally hits your clit on the way down. I lean against the table, still trying to compose myself. You sit up, scoot over to where I am, and taking my face in your hands, give me a tender, soulful kiss. "I need to come to school more often," you say.

Water Sports

"Jody" is twenty-six and lives in Atlanta, Georgia. He spends at least two weeks every winter on Key Biscayne, where, he says, one day he intends to move full-time to pursue his two favorite hobbies.

I love to water ski and fuck. Not necessarily in that order—but almost. My fantasy combines both. I've been hired by a lovely French woman, a tourist visiting Miami for a week, to teach her how to water ski.

She's stunning, tall and thin with large shoulders that accentuate her narrow waist and well-shaped breasts. She must have brought a suitcase full of different sexy swimsuits.

Monique is a great student. She's up on the skis like a pro within a half-hour. By noon I've had her on a single slalom ski, wake jumping and doing all sorts of stunts. We break for lunch and while we're eating by the pool of her rented villa overlooking Biscayne Bay, I tell her that in the afternoon, since I've outrun the curriculum, I'll have to teach her to have sex on skis. Monique laughs, finishes her glass of wine and says, "Let's go."

I have Freddie, the guy who I use to skipper the powerboat, position it off the end of the dock. I tell Monique that we'll sit on the edge of the dock, holding the tow rope, and he'll pull us off sharing one set of skis. She nods and I have Monique climb on my lap, we signal Freddie, who guns it, and away we go.

Monique leans back into me as we accelerate, and feeling her ass against my balls gives me a hard-on. She immediately notices the erection and grinds her ass against me. I hold the tow bar in one hand and slip my hand down the front of her bikini bottom and fondle her pussy. She reaches behind her and rubs my cock. We are rocketing along Biscayne Bay. I have three fingers in Monique's vagina. I slide them in and out. The vibration from the skis slapping the surface of the water is really getting to her.

She stops rubbing my cock and with one hand pulls down on my swimming trucks until they're at about midthigh and then does the same with hers.

H i s   S e c r e t   L i f e   *163*

I move my left arm so that she can lean forward on it, and as she does she takes my cock and inserts it between her legs from behind.

We're zooming along, cutting in and out among the sailboats. Monique has gone limp so that I can control the balance for both of us. As I twist and turn and jump and maneuver, I'm driving my cock in and out. We ski that way for a half-hour. Freddie is really piling on the coals and I start jumping the wake, back and forth, faster and faster. Monique moans every time we land. I hear her cry, "now, now, now." I come and so does she. It's a miracle that we're still on the skis! I drop the rope and we glide to a stop and sink into the water, my cock still in her.

We disengage. As Freddie brings the boat around Monique removes her suit and I do the same. We toss them to Freddie, who leers and says we probably were responsible for three capsizings and a head-on collision. Make that a hard-on collision. We paddle around the boat for a while. Monique swims to the ladder and as I come over she kisses me. She faces me with her back to the ladder. I hold on to the side rails with my feet on the bottom rung. Monique wraps her legs around my waist and we screw again, half in and half out of the water. Freddie turns up the radio so that he doesn't have to listen to the noise.

Men crave positive reinforcement. There's always a niggling doubt that maybe he's not quite an eleven-plus on a ten-point scale of excellence. But the insecurity tends to vanish when his fantasy lover is willing to have sex with him on water skis in the middle of Biscayne Bay. He must be doing something right! In the world of fantasy, you can do everything right.

There is, I would think, a large helping of exhibitionism involved in these fantasies. A genuine exhibitionist, of the flasher variety, is so filled with self-doubt about his own worth and sexuality that he needs to provoke a response from the strangers he confronts: She blanched, therefore I am.

Milder forms of exhibitionism reflect the same need but on a correspondingly reduced level. The fantasizer who is imagining sex in public scenarios is saying in effect: "If it just so happens that you notice me making love with this gorgeous woman in the back of my van in the mall parking lot, you'll realize how powerfully attractive I really am."

And since this is a fantasy, not reality, the ego reinforcement is self-generated and not purchased at someone else's expense. What I think is easily overlooked is the battering that male and female self-esteem take in the course of everyday life. The world tends to be a harsh and unforgiving place. By the time a person reaches the age of twenty or twenty-five, he or she has usually mastered a basic set of coping skills. Among these are little survival tricks like going on shopping sprees to fight a bout of depression or driving like a maniac to get the adrenaline flowing again. Likewise, sex and sexuality are used to alter moods and counteract the vicissitudes of life.

Some of this—particularly sex as Prozac—can be ugly and hurtful. Promiscuousness and so-called "sex addictions" are symptoms of both deep psychological troubles and the tendency to self-medicate these painful afflictions using whatever resources are available. Like someone who overeats to generate a feeling of contentment, people who attempt to copulate their way to happiness are desperately seeking remedies that, in the end, are self-destructive.

I see fantasy as an alternative to sex as Prozac. In moderate doses and kept in perspective, it amounts to a couple of aspirins. A ten-minute sex-in-public fantasy is no miracle cure for a guy who's lost his job, had his car repossessed, been bitten by his dog and can't get a date. But it is a little "just in time" triage that will probably get him through the day.

Part III

Beyond Ground Zero

Ten

Secret Compromises: Oral Sex

When I told a friend of mine that I was writing a book about male fantasies, she nodded and said, "A book about blow jobs, eh?"

Not quite. Though I do have to acknowledge that oral sex holds a powerful attraction to most men. It is a theme or a component part of many fantasies. That's not surprising. Most recent sex surveys show that oral sex is appealing to roughly 80 percent of all young and middle-aged men (the figure falls off for older men but stays above 60 percent). In the *Sex in America* study that came out in 1994, only watching your partner undress (number two) and vaginal intercourse (number one) were more popular.*

I really don't think there's much of a mystery here that needs explaining. The male genitalia are a bundle of relatively easily stimulated nerve endings. Arousal by way of a partner's lips, tongue and mouth

*Sex in America: A Definitive Survey, by Robert T. Michael, John H. Gagnon, Edward O. Laumann, and Gina Kolata (Boston: Little, Brown and Company, 1994).

closely duplicates that which occurs during vaginal intercourse. But there are added attractions. The tongue is more agile than vaginal muscles, for one thing. Being the recipient of oral sex, for another, rather than the provider of penetration during vaginal intercourse, gives a man the closest thing to a free ride that he is ever likely to receive during the course of his sex life.

I think it is this factor of having someone else responsible for punching the buttons that makes oral sex so appealing. It brings us back to the concept that men are searching for ways to escape from traditional sexual roles. Oral sex is the perfect route in that it provides orgasm without penetration.

For centuries—*many* millennia is probably more accurate—the starting point of the male sexual paradigm has been: The penis enters the vagina. It has been the fundamental definition of male sexuality and sexual satisfaction. Oral sex and masturbation, which we will discuss in the next chapter, violate that norm and there were powerful taboos against both practices.

In talking to sexologists, I've learned that intercourse serves at least two purposes, historically: Procreation and emotional bonding, which contributes to the survival possibilities of the offspring by encouraging the mother and father to combine their labor and nurturing abilities in the face of a hostile environment. Oral sex doesn't contribute to either imperative.

The *Sex in America* survey found that among women aged eighteen to forty-four only 19 percent regarded giving oral sex as very appealing. Fifty percent of the men, in the same age category, rated it that way. Perhaps a more telling statistic was that 43 percent of the women find giving oral sex to be not appealing or, the strongest category of aversion, not at all appealing. The figure goes up by another 26 percent among older women, forty-five to fifty-nine years old.

The divide between men and women on the subject of oral sex lends itself to being bridged by fantasy. And bridged it is. Close to half the fantasies I collected for this book involved some degree of oral sex, though it may not have been the dominant theme.

Given the survey figures, the attraction of the oral-sex fantasy is obvious. Most men have to realize that their interest in oral sex poses a potential conflict with their lovers, or, if not an overt conflict, a disparity in sexual satisfaction. In a fantasy that is just not an issue. There's no negotiation, no compromise, no sense of grievance or obligation, either before or after the act.

The fantasy performs its classic role as safety valve and possibly provides the missing ingredients of a satisfactory sex life.

Above all else, oral sex in a fantasy is there when a man wants it. The risk of complications or rejection has been removed. He doesn't even have to ask—it just happens.

Water Power

"J.C." is twenty-five years old. He lives north of San Francisco, where he restores and sells classic Austin-Healey sports cars. He tells us that he has been in a relationship for two months, which "is somewhat serious, but definitely monogamous."

> *I'm* on a mountaintop in the countryside with my girl-friend where we have discovered a waterfall. We lie on the ground, so close to the waterfall that it's almost crashing down onto us.
>
> As the water begins to wash up against our flesh, she leans over to me and starts to kiss me as her hands roam up and down my thighs.
>
> She moves down my body, slowly, and licks the droplets of water off my skin and kisses me ever so softly and sensually. I feel the heat of her breath every time she lays a kiss on

my skin and the closer she gets to my genitals, the more aroused I am. She moves down on me and kisses the area of my inner thighs and strokes my penis, up and down the entire length of it.

She licks the area around my penis, and my hard-on is dying to be inside her mouth, until in one quick motion, she takes all of me in and gently sucks on my penis, kneading it with her lips. She takes her tongue and licks me on the tip of my penis, which is particularly arousing, and then slides me in and out of her mouth.

When she can feel that I'm about to explode in her mouth, she releases my penis and deftly slides into the water, gliding under the waterfall. I dive in and go after her. We begin to kiss as we drift up onto the gravel bank, propelled by the pressure of the waterfall. She climbs on top of me and I slide right into her. She rocks back and forth on top of me, and the harder I grab her breasts, the faster the pace becomes. After a few minutes of her grinding against me, and the roughness of the gravel on my ass, I flip her around onto her knees with her palms up against the trunk of a tree. The cheeks of her ass are staring boldly at me, ready for penetration. I move against her and put my hard-on inside her and thrust quickly in and out.

I swing my arms around to her front and stimulate her clit with my fingers as I move in and out of her tight ass. Her body begins to shake against mine and the two of us are overcome by these wavelike currents as the juices flow down into the water and wash away.

The *Sex in America* survey sheds some light on an element in this fantasy, anal intercourse, which also has occurred in several of the other scenarios in this book so far. Ninety-six percent of younger women found passive anal intercourse to be not appealing or not at all appealing. Almost 15 percent of the men had the opposite reaction and found active anal intercourse to be very appealing or somewhat appealing.

Even more than oral sex, anal intercourse is a minefield of potential conflicts between lovers if a man is interested in this practice. The recurrence of this fantasy element suggests to me that it is fulfilling the function of providing a taste of "exotic" sex that is not usually available.

Sexual curiosity isn't exhausted during the teenage years for males when first experiences and experiments take place. Wondering what it's like to have anal intercourse, or any of the other acts that one's partner is reluctant to perform, is perfectly natural. The fantasy acts as an introductory course—anal intercourse 101.

I've always suspected that many men fear that they are the only guy in the world who isn't getting any oral sex, anal sex, group sex—you name it. Fantasies are a way to join "the team."

Window Shopping

"Dale" is forty-one. He lives in Missoula, Montana, where he practices law.

> *I* am taking a walk during my lunch break. I decide to stroll through a part of town I do not usually visit. As I am looking in various shop windows, I notice a tall girl with dark blonde hair, around twenty-two years old, working alone in a shoe store. She is on the phone behind a glass counter.
>
> I get a good look at her: she is wearing a black miniskirt, high heels and a low-cut, V-neck–type sweater. She has an incredible figure. Long beautiful legs, thin waist, shapely breasts, long slender arms, gorgeous young face with blue eyes, a luscious mouth and incredible hair. I watch her for a little while and then I decide to walk in.

She gets off the telephone and comes over to me and asks if I need help. She smiles very sweetly as though she knows me from somewhere. I point out a pair of shoes and she goes to the back room for them.

She comes back with the shoebox and sits down in front of me. Her beautiful long legs straddle the small seat and her miniskirt raises to just below her crotch. She is busy putting on my shoes so I take the opportunity to check out as much of her legs and the rest of her body as possible. I can see clearly that she's wearing a black G-string under her short skirt. She must be quite well-shaved down there because the G-string does not cover much territory.

She looks up at me quickly and notices my eyes glancing at her crotch. She smiles at me sweetly and asks, "What do you think?" I ask her, "About the shoes?" Before she has a chance to respond, I tell her that they are too loose and ask if there's anything "a little tighter." She says she'll have to go in the back room and look.

She returns a few minutes later and asks if I would mind holding the ladder for her because the shoes I want are on the top shelf and she is working alone. So we go back to the stockroom and she slides the ladder over into position. As I hold it steady she climbs to the top. At this point I can see everything. Her G-string is riding up on her beautiful firm ass. She is bent over letting me see it all. She pulls out a shoebox and climbs down the ladder.

I can tell by the look on her face that she is enjoying this seduction. She is extremely sexy and knows it. She is an expert on how to tease men and make them wild. She is young and just beginning to explore the power she can generate with her sexuality. I'm enjoying the seduction as much as she is.

The telephone rings. She picks up the phone in the back room next to the ladder. It appears to be a friend of hers on the line. A woman friend. She laughs and quietly whispers into the telephone that she is in the back room right now with a very handsome stranger. As she says this she looks over at me and smiles. She positions herself on the ladder so that she can cross her legs and remove her shoes. She starts to rub her foot, then her ankle, then works her way up her leg. "Yes, he's here right now, and he's really cute!" She is talking very softly on the phone and looking at me, smiling. "I don't know, I'll ask him," she says, holding out the phone receiver. "My friend would like to talk to you. Is that okay?" I take the phone and hear a voice that drips with sex appeal: "My friend tells me you are really cute. You know what? I think she's hot for you. She told me that she would really like to take down your pants and suck your hot cock right now."

I'm listening to this over the phone, and as if that were not enough, this lovely creature of a salesgirl next to me is sliding up her skirt, spreading her legs and starting to finger herself. Then she moves her hands over to me and slowly slides them up my thighs and starts to massage my crotch. While this is happening, I'm listening to the voice over the phone telling me that not only is the girl in the shoe store hot for me, but she, too, has a few things in mind that she would like to do to me.

At this point, the salesgirl has unzipped my fly and is fumbling around for my quickly hardening penis. She takes it out and starts to draw her lush lips close. "Ahhh," says the voice on the phone, "my pussy is so wet for you. And my clit is so hot. I want your dick up my pussy right now. I've got to have you."

Her lips wrap around my penis, sucking me into her mouth further than I have ever been sucked before. I am dizzy with excitement. Either one of these two events would be enough to get me off, but the two together—sensational!

"Oh, come over here and fuck me, I want you right now. I want to feel your stiff dick up my ass. Slide your cock up into my beautiful tight ass." Meanwhile, in the shoe store, I'm getting sucked deeper and deeper, while she fingers herself. She stops, turns around, and lifts up her miniskirt and sticks her head and upper torso between two rungs of the ladder. This move reveals a marvelous ass at the end of those lean legs. "Do it the back way," she says, as she arches her ass way into the air. "I love it up the ass."

The whole thing is almost too much for me to comprehend. Here is this gorgeous girl bent over the ladder with her ass staring me in the face and my hard dick moving in and out of her asshole. Simultaneously, this voice on the other end of the phone is breathing more and more heavily. As my fucking increases in speed, the shoe store girl starts to scream with pleasure. The girl on the phone is turned on by the sound and starts to scream as well. The entire scene escalates into a wild, three-way orgasm. My juices shoot all over her back. The girl on the phone screams her head off for about a minute. The shoe store girl, totally satisfied, turns over on her back, slumps to the foot of the ladder and smiles.

I tell the girl on the phone and the salesgirl that I have to get back to work. thanks a lot and maybe we can all get together some time in person. Both of them agree that we must do it again sometime, and I leave the store.

Roman Holiday

"Craig" is forty-eight and "holding." Married with one child, he lives in Montclair, New Jersey, and is a mathematician with an internationally known research lab.

I'm flying tourist-class from New York to Rome for a vacation. I'm in the window seat, the middle is empty and the aisle is occupied by an Italian woman who looks to be around twenty. I try to engage in conversation with her, but she apparently doesn't speak English. I attempt some pidgin Italian but give up and tell her that I'm lucky to be traveling with such a beautiful lady.

After dinner and the movie I tuck a pillow under my head and go to sleep. My seatmate does the same. I doze off but soon realize that something or someone is leaning on my shoulder. I open my eyes and see that she has slumped across the middle seat and ended up leaning against me. I can smell her perfume and clean hair. As I'm savoring the situation, she slowly slips down my chest and her head comes to rest on my lap. The plane is pretty empty but I don't relish the idea of being observed so I cover the two of us with a blanket.

I feel a hand on my thigh, stroking it slowly. My prick turns to stone immediately and I can feel it pressing against her cheek. The hand moves between my legs and cups my balls, then up to the zipper in the trousers. Down it comes. She unbuckles the belt and I can feel my cock spring upright.

My seatmate doesn't move her lower body at all. She appears to be sound asleep. But her hand is moving, up and down the shaft of my cock. I'm starting to breathe hard as the stewardess stops and asks if she can get me anything. My eyes are wide open so I can't pretend to be asleep. "No, no . . . I'm fine," I say, barely able to croak out the words. She leaves and my cock slides down the throat of a lady whose name I don't know.

She is a genuine sword swallower. She sucks and tongues me for fifteen minutes, at least, and never seems to have to come up for air. I fight my orgasm off as long as I can, but finally I just let go. The Italian woman continues sucking and tonguing throughout. When I'm dry, she releases my cock and her head goes still. I lie there stunned and then fall asleep.

The next thing I know the cabin crew is handing out breakfast trays. My seatmate is back in her own place, sipping coffee and eating a buttered roll. In between bites, she is reading a paperback. I don't remember the title but it was in English.

Although it is "better to give than receive," I don't know how many men would actually subscribe to the "better" part of the old admonition. The surveys show that receiving oral sex has the edge over giving it by approximately 10 percent.

The figure surprises me, frankly. When I talk to men about sex, I pick up strong vibes that many of them are squeamish about giving oral sex to their female partners. My advice to them, borrowed from Mayor Marion Barry of Washington, D.C., is "Get over it." Nearly 70 percent of younger women are telling survey researchers that they like receiving oral sex.

Fellatio and cunnilingus now seem to be linked and men are going to find it increasingly difficult to ignore the Golden Rule when it comes to oral sex. "Do unto me and I'll owe you one" (the gold-plated rule)—doesn't cut it. Many oral-sex fantasies seem to recognize this and cunnilingus is incorporated into foreplay. Most men take their responsibilities as lovers seriously. They want to satisfy their partners. If giving oral sex is a means to that end—then oral sex it is.

The Ordinary Extraordinary

"Simon" is thirty years old. He lives in Pittsburgh, Pennsylvania, where he manages a valet-parking operation for parties and special events.

My fantasy starts out as an ordinary night with my girl-friend and ends up as something special! We start with a lit-tle kissing. Not just the face, but all over the body, starting with the face but moving down to the toes, stripping off pieces of clothing as we come to them.

I lower myself onto her and plunge my tongue inside. I reach my arms up and fondle her breasts at the same time. She tastes so sweet and I really enjoy pleasing her. After I tease her clitoris with my tongue, she starts coming in small spurts. I move up along her body and she starts passionately kissing me. I wrap my arms around her and flip her onto the bed so that she will be on top of me. I love looking at her and the feeling I get when she's on top, as if she is surrounding me.

I lift her up and she comes right down onto me and takes my penis inside her. I reach up and grab her breasts and start to move them around in my hands. She gets to rocking and rolling back and forth on top of me with her back arched. I'm dying to come but won't allow myself—the feeling is too good to let go of too soon.

I grab her hips and make her slow down just a bit so that I don't come so quickly. But she forces my hands free and starts grinding against me. I can't control it a second longer and I come inside her. She collapses into my arms and we stay that way for a while.

Just Desserts

"Marty" is a twenty-four-year-old tractor-trailer driver. He told us, "I'm not in a relationship at the moment and I'm not necessarily look-ing for one." But he adds, "However, I wouldn't mind having someone to hang out with."

I go out to eat with this girl I'm seeing. We have about three bottles of wine during the meal, which turns into some crazy foreplay. She removes her shoe underneath the table and begins to massage my penis with her foot. She is very calm in what she is doing, unlike me—I'm looking all around to see if anyone notices. I must say that she is bring-ing me a lot of pleasure, and the outline of my hard-on is completely visible through my slacks. I'm trying to rub it down with my elbow but it keeps bouncing up.

We ask for the check before the meal even arrives and race back to my place. I turn on the tube and we lie on the couch side by side.

She takes her hands and begins to stroke me over my pants while I kiss her. I put my tongue inside her mouth while she rubs my hard-on into this altered state of numb-ness. I need her more than ever. She begins to take her clothes off and then she helps me with mine, using her mouth and teeth. I lower myself down her body and put my tongue inside her warm, sweet cunt. She is so wet that I can't wait to slide it right in. She shifts her body onto mine so that I can still eat her out and she, too, can indulge in tasting me.

She slides her mouth over my penis and begins to draw me in and out of her. My hard-on grows in her mouth until I can't take it anymore. I throw her against the couch and begin to drive it in from behind. I can hear my balls slapping against her ass, and the moans from the pleasure she is getting fire me up more and more. I drill my prick into her deeper and deeper.

I swing my arms around her and take her breasts into my hands, molding and shaping them as I see fit. I need to see her huge breasts, so I lie down on the ground and throw her onto my joystick, grabbing her hips and moving her back and forth.

She begins to jump up and down on me, not knowing what to do with all the pleasure she is getting. I grab her by the hips again and give her the direction that she needs, and the steadiness I need.

After countless minutes of complete fucking, groping and animal instincts, we both come together and take a five-minute break before we start all over again.

The Medium Is the Massage

"Asa" is fifty-one years old. He's married (for the second time) and lives in Georgia where he does computer consulting and some real-estate appraising.

I'm in a restaurant with a lady friend I really desire. She is dressed like a slut: tight skirt, lots of makeup, the whole bit. The evening begins slowly with a romantic aura. We drink some wine, dance a little and generally set and foreshadow the entire sexual scenario. After dinner we go to a motel room. As soon as I close the door she's on me, rubbing against me like a cat. She initiates the whole thing.

I slide my hand underneath her shirt and start to caress the area around her nipples. We tease one another with soft kisses all over the body, barely touching each other's skin as we move up and down. I can feel her breath on my neck, my chest, my thighs, and it is extremely arousing.

We lie on the bed and start to give one another total body massages. I'm massaging her all over except where she most wants it. She keeps pushing my hand toward her vagina but I'm resisting, teasing her. I lower my face to her body and start to kiss and lick the area around her upper and inner thighs. She is pushing my head toward her but I keep pulling back. After a few short cries, I jam my tongue inside her and feel her wetness. She holds my head in place as I taste her.

I am totally submerged in satisfying her. Her moaning is arousing me to the limit, so I continue to orally stimulate her as I rub my hard-on at the same time. She pulls me up and unzips me. She sticks her hands in my boxers and pulls me out. I slide right into her. She puts her hands on my ass and is pushing me down onto her, making my impact stronger and stronger. Just as I encounter that riding-the-wave feeling, I pull out and turn her around. I put myself in her from the rear, and the visual aspect of it is totally exciting me.

After a moment or two of intense penetration, and my balls smacking against her ass, I come inside her and all over the back side of her body.

On the Rocks

"Klaus" describes himself as a thirty-three-year-old phone sex operator, living in Florida. He is single and not in a current relationship.

There is a corporate-looking woman, someone who is definitely in charge. She is wearing a business suit and is completely the New York type. She's a bit older than me, in her late thirties or early forties. I go and see her for a job interview.

She gives me an application to fill out and a written mini exam, and then assesses me right then and there. As she looks over my exam, I go to the refrigerator and get some ice cubes. Her eyes are following me as I cross the room. I come back and sit in front of her as I slide the ice cubes in and out of my mouth.

She looks at me and says, "Unfortunately, you're not qualified," as she slides her legs up onto the top of the desk and spreads them wide. She is not wearing any underwear and I have a great view of her vagina. I take one of the ice cubes from my mouth and touch her ankle with it to see how she responds. She arches her back and slides back into the chair. I know it is safe.

I take the ice cube and start to travel up the length of her inner thigh. As she opens her legs further apart, I go behind her and swing her chair around and force her legs to straddle over each arm of the chair. I put an ice cube in my mouth and start to kiss her inner thighs.

I open the jacket to her suit and drip water on her nipples and stomach. I put her breasts in my mouth and suck on them. I move down on her body and start to stimulate her clit with my tongue. I put the ice cube inside her vagina and push it with my tongue.

She grabs my face and pushes it against her wetness. I am licking her all up. The moaning is driving me crazy and she finally secretes a sweet fluid as her body jerks and trembles in the chair. She goes down on the floor and makes me lie down with her. She begins to tongue me and takes one of the ice cubes from my mouth and puts it in hers. She goes down my body and takes my penis out, sliding her cold tongue up and down my shaft. She takes me inside her mouth and slides the cold water down my penis, as she wets my balls with another ice cube.

She climbs on top of me and puts my cold, hard penis inside of her. She starts rocking back and forth, as I circle her nipples with my icy hands. I take them in my fingers and twist and turn them. She rides me back and forth. I grab her hips and help her move faster and faster on top of me.

She is moaning and screaming as her breasts whack me back and forth in the face. As she comes, her body shakes on top of mine and begins to slow down, but I need her more than ever at the moment. I take her ass into my hands and lift her up and down until she is pouncing like a maniac on my hard-on and the impact makes me erupt into her.

Maybe . . . just maybe, giving and receiving oral sex amounts to a set of training wheels attached to the new sexuality. Oral sex shows up in so many fantasy scenarios that it is clearly part of the mainstream these days, whereas forty or fifty years ago it was apparently not a standard part of the repertoire of most couples.

One of its chief characteristics is that vaginal penetration is not involved, and for men to take to oral sex as enthusiastically as they have indicates that the door has been opened to a redefined sexuality as opposed to the traditional "slam, bam, thank you, Ma'am" techniques that have caused such anger, anguish and frustration among women.

I wouldn't be so sanguine, though, if we were only talking about fellatio, which, next to masturbation, is about as self-centered a sex act as there is. But younger women in increasing numbers are beginning to enjoy and expect to receive oral sex from their partners. If nothing else, it is probably the best thing to happen to foreplay since the invention of the French kiss.

Equal time for oral sex takes time. It prolongs lovemaking. By slowing the whole process—the rush to ejaculation—men are becoming acquainted with the joy of unhurried sex. These fantasies tell me that there is so much pleasure in oral sex—giving and receiving—that they are willing to delay orgasm.

While most of the scenarios also included vaginal intercourse, they start to read like smorgasbords that could easily lose a few courses and still provide a decent meal. I'd like to think that we're headed for a day when the alternatives to intercourse are so attractive that they fully satisfy and that opting for them is perfectly natural. As it is now, we almost have to seek permission or come up with an excuse not to "go all the way."

Male and female genitals are still ground zero of the human erogenous zones, but oral sex is teaching us that there is other territory that's worth exploring—slowly.

One last, uncomfortable word about fellatio—swallowing. None of the fantasies in this chapter and few others in the book make much of the issue of women swallowing male semen. I've got to say that I would have predicted otherwise when I started this project.

In talking to men about oral sex, I got the impression that swallowing is an important part of fellatio. I said as much on the air one night when Dr. June Reinish of the Kinsey Institute adroitly turned the tables on me when I asked her why men like women to swallow. She said, "I don't know Bob, why do men like to swallow?" I was left sitting there doing a Ralph Kramden imitation—"Humma, humma, humma . . ." The best I could do was suggest that for men it brought the act to closure. And research by sexologists does show that many men do expect it or at least find it gratifying.

But to play fair with the analysis of these fantasies, I wonder whether it is, indeed, all that important. If what you see is what you get, we're not seeing it in the fantasies. Perhaps in this age of negotiation and compromise, men are realizing that oral sex that doesn't come to closure is better than no oral sex at all.

Eleven

Secrets of Shame: Men and Masturbation

My guess is that less has been written about masturbation in recent years than any other erotic subject. Foot fetishism gets more press.

The masturbation blackout is odd. What is probably the most frequently practiced form of male sexual gratification ends up being the least examined and celebrated.

It's too bad. Masturbation deserves better, and should be dealt with in a manner appropriate to a serious, legitimate and adult sexual prerogative.

Most sex surveys find that well over 60 percent of all adult males regard masturbation as a natural part of their sex lives. And I happen to think that 60 percent is a conservative figure. I'd put it around 80 percent. It's not a question of abstinence.

Does he or doesn't he? He does. Men just don't freely acknowledge that they are engaging in regular masturbation.

Some of this reticence is the effect of a lingering taboo. It wasn't all that many years ago that sex education tracts and "personal hygiene" advice admonished boys and girls to keep their hands off their genitals.

The *slightly* exaggerated consequences of ignoring the warnings ranged from chronic illness to stunted growth, sterility to depravity, nearsightedness to thumb-sucking and hairy palms to, horror of horrors—"Your pecker will drop off."

Take it from me, and I speak from personal experience: It won't. Fortunately that doesn't come as big news to most men. The authors of the *Janus Report* found that 55 percent of the men they surveyed acknowledged regularly masturbating anywhere from daily to monthly.* The figures, by the way, also show that 19 percent said they "never" masturbate. If we factor in those who are too ashamed to admit to the practice and those who may be suffering an illness, the voluntary nonmasturbators are a tiny minority. Truly, in this case, there is a huge "silent majority."

As a sex act, masturbation is about as benign as it gets. A society determined to avoid teenage pregnancy, the spread of AIDS and antisocial sexual behavior would seem better advised to encourage masturbation among sexually active males (and females) than to discourage it. Apparently, former surgeon general Jocelyn Elders thought so too, but a passing positive comment on the subject in 1994 almost instantaneously cost her her job.

My feeling is that there is strong prejudice against sex that is nonprocreative. The prehistoric need to expand family and tribal numbers and to impose social stability led to the stigmatization of sex that was solely a matter of personal pleasure.

There's more to it than that, though. Onanism, the term the anti-masturbation zealots of the eighteenth century hung on the practice, derives from the Old Testament story of Onan, the son of Judah who practiced a form of birth control that today we call coitus interruptus. Back then it was known as "spilling thy seed on barren ground."

The Janus Report on Sexual Behavior, by Samuel S. Janus, Ph.D., and Cynthia L. Janus, M.D. (New York: John Wiley & Sons, 1993).

Bad press is one thing, getting bad press in the Bible is another. "Let thy penis go!"

In 1741, a Swiss quack by the name of S. A. D. Tissot wrote a pamphlet titled "Onanism, or a Treatise on the Disorders of Masturbation." Tissot was a crackpot who claimed that masturbation robbed the body of essential fluids and opened the way for chronic diseases and mental illness.

It wasn't long before other pseudoscientific and medical entrepreneurs climbed on the bandwagon. Tissot's disciples linked masturbation to epilepsy, tuberculosis and nearsightedness. Before long, masturbators could be picked out of a crowd by their debilitated and feeble appearance. It's been said that Charles Dickens's physical description of Uriah Heep in the novel *David Copperfield* is meant to signal the reader that the deceitful and unctuous character was a masturbator.

But don't blame it on Dickens or poor old Queen Victoria. Culture was at war with most forms of sexual pleasure long before primitive Britons stopped painting themselves blue. (When I ride the tube in London, I often wonder if they haven't resumed the practice.)

I think masturbation continued to be regarded as a subversive act because it was seen as a powerful inducement to men to withdraw from their role as husbands, fathers and, according to some theories, soldiers energized to fight and kill by their bottled-up sexual tension. (There are also scholars who believe that homosexual intimacy between military comrades was used by the ancient Greeks to create loyalty and inspire lovers to battle to the death on one another's behalf.) Basically, masturbation was feared on the grounds that it robbed coupled sex of its magic power.

There probably would have been laws against masturbation if anyone could have figured out a way to enforce them. Relations between the sexes are far more easily subjected to ceremonies, licensing and prohibitions by the government. When more than one person is involved, someone can always turn state's evidence. But as for a boy and his penis, there's a lot of deniability and there weren't many suitable punishment options when a culprit was caught in the act.

Cutting off Billy Bob's hands meant that he wouldn't be available for a day's work. Wet dreams and a good imagination can thwart the most intricate male chastity belts.

What could the enemies of Onanism do? Issue dire warnings, and—what else—make a profit. J. H. Kellogg, probably as much a quack as Tissot, invented cornflakes to cure masturbation, which was a damned sight better than some of his other ideas, among them circumcising boys without anesthesia and dosing a girl's clitoris in carbolic acid.

Fortunately, selling cornflakes was a lot easier and more lucrative. So the only thing to do was to scare the young lad (males were still the chief culprits) with tall tales about going cross-eyed, losing his memory, or "running out of bullets in his gun."

Nice try. But it didn't work all that well. Instead of putting a stop to masturbation it drove it underground. When they were alone, Billy Bob and his brothers continued to take matters into their own hands. And they felt rotten about it. Not only were they risking insanity and defying Mom and Dad, they were getting entangled in the elaborate psychological web that Freud identified with his work concerning early childhood toilet training.

Without delving too deeply into Freudian concepts, let me say this: When it comes to what the godfather of modern psychotherapy regarded as the giving and withholding of feces, urine or semen, it is *all about* the ferocious personal battle for control between a child and his or her parents. The taboo against masturbation uses many of the techniques of enforcement that parents wield during toilet training—rewards, punishment and, most of all, shame. Dirty diapers and sticky sheets end up meaning the same thing—you're a bad boy.

And that's the *real* shame. Masturbation, a perfectly natural part of sexuality, is reduced to the status of defecation and urination, the voiding of bodily waste products. Billy Bob must learn to control his bowels, his bladder and his prostate or be written off as a slob.

No wonder that masturbation becomes men's first sexual secret, and for many of us, the last. We'll blab about bondage and free associate about fetishes and fantasies, but go silent when the subject turns to masturbation. On my desk, I have the stack of questionnaires I collected in the last few years from men about their sexuality. The candor is amazing. Still, only about one in ten even mentions masturbation.

Most frequently, it's a postscript. A guy will relate a torrid story and then conclude with, "That's about all for today. I'm going to go jerk off."

This aspect of masturbation—the quick and easy release of sexual tension—is one reason why it is a common practice, as well as one that is regarded with a substantial amount of squeamishness. To many men, masturbation has no mystique or romance attached to it. Close the door, unzip, grab your penis. Get it over with. Don't get caught.

Speed and stealth are prerequisites for adolescent boys hiding their masturbatory activities from their mothers. The habit is hard to break. What's easier is coming up with the rationalization that masturbation is just another bodily function that doesn't deserve much time, effort or imagination.

But imagination is inextricably linked to masturbation. Many fantasies do, in fact, end with masturbation, as men seek to vent the sexual tension they've created. And that's what my correspondents are saying when they add the "I think I'll go jerk off" postscript to the questionnaires. The addenda are so studied in their casualness that I wonder if it doesn't indicate a deliberate effort, and probably an unsuccessful one, to strip masturbation of its shame.

The other way it's presented in the questionnaires that suggests there is a subliminal message involved is as a guilty secret discovered by a mother, wife or girlfriend. Usually, there's a lot of initial embarrassment. One man wrote, as part of a fantasy set in a doctor's office:

"You must pound it real hard and often," the nurse said when she noticed the red welts on my dick. I stammered and stuttered. I didn't know what to say.

She smiled at me. "Show me your technique. I love to watch."

First, shame. Then, permission. This fantasy, and others like it, is a way to realize a desire that may be impossible to fulfill in real life. He fears being caught, but actually wants to be exposed because then the secret will be revealed and sanctioned.

That word again—sanctioned.

It's exactly what men do when they treat masturbation like a bodily function. They're giving themselves permission. There's no choice in the matter, and therefore no guilt.

Another way to remove the onus is to treat masturbation like an illness. To paraphrase comedian Flip Wilson, "Here come d'nurse."

The nurse is a favorite fantasy character for men, right up there with cheerleaders and prostitutes. The imaginary heirs of Florence Nightingale get involved in everything from toe sucking to "golden showers." I think it's the combination of an authority figure, like Mom, with the reality of a worldly, take-charge woman. Here's another example of a fantasy, from "Wallace," and in it masturbation is presented as a disease that needs to be cured.

I am a patient in a sex clinic, under treatment for chronic masturbation. She is a nurse who ties me kneeling across a chair in order to deliver "genital therapy" for my condition.

My hands and knees are bound to the leg of the chair, and I am completely helpless. My thighs are tied well apart, and I can look back at my naked genitals dangling vulnerably and defenselessly between my legs. She begins by lightly tickling my penis to erection, and she explains, "The purpose of genital therapy is to manually bring the patient just to the brink of climax, then withdraw all stimulation. Repeated applications eventually teach the patient to deal with frustrated sexual urges and wean him from his abnormal habits."

What strikes me here is the juxtaposition of perceived abnormality with the intense pleasure he obviously derives from masturbation. The fantasy continues:

She warns me that I will feel intense pressures, and that I may say and shout things that later will cause me embarrassment, but she will understand how I am feeling, and urges me to say whatever I feel like. As she masturbates me again and again to the precipice of orgasm with deliberate cruel slowness, only to withdraw at the last second, I cry, plead, beg for relief, for her to finish me off. But she is pitiless, and only begins to torment my manhood.

When I become too excited and threaten to relieve my tension through my own writhing in my bonds, she takes corrective measures by spanking my upturned buttocks or— as a last resort—lightly stroking my testicles (creating a mild, aching sensation that can be very stimulating. Of course, a little goes a long way.) It is the ultimate symbol of dominant female power to have these precious treasures of masculinity punished by a flick of her fingers.

She even threatens, if I fail to respond to treatments, to have me castrated, since the "therapeutic" castration is preferable to the ravages resulting from chronic self-abuse.

There's an element here of dominance and submission, which we'll leave for another chapter, but the abnormality-pleasure-punishment equation is something that occurs frequently when masturbation is at issue, according to many sex therapists.

I think it reflects not only shame generated by transgressing a still-powerful taboo but also a breach of the male contract. By masturbating—or committing "chronic self-abuse"—he is not doing his job of being an effective lover with a female partner.

If nothing else, men are creatures of cause and effect. They see their role in the sex act as the cause of their partner's pleasure and, therefore, their ego is satisfied by the effect—"I made her happy."

Under those terms, masturbation is essentially a selfish act. I made myself happy. And there's absolutely nothing—nothing—wrong with that. But coming to terms with sexual pleasure for the sake of pleasure, pleasure without apologies or hang-ups, is a notion that still makes many of us acutely uncomfortable.

I suspect that the common nurse-masturbation fantasies not only give men permission to masturbate without guilt—it's therapeutic, after all—but also fulfills the desire to involve another person, via the fantasy, in the tidal wave of pleasure generated by masturbation.

Demonstration Projects

A fifty-six-year-old man by the name of "Lyle" provided me with a fantasy-reality scenario that reflects the desire to break out of the isolation of masturbation and share the pleasure.

For a long time, I used to fantasize about having a woman watch me masturbate. It took me years to pluck up the courage to do it. First, it was with my wife, and I got so hard and excited that when I came, I ejaculated two feet into the air. She was impressed, if not puzzled. Now she's quite used to it and I masturbate in front of her quite often. I have to be naked, by the way, as the feeling of absolute nakedness is crucial to my enjoyment.

I made a video of me masturbating. It got me so turned

on and produced such an impressive come shot that even more than a year later, when I watch it, I get hard in seconds and come within a minute.

I fantasize about being in a porn movie. In the opening scene, I'd shave my pubic hair and masturbate. Knowing all those people were watching, I'd produce such legendary come, I'd be famous and men all over the world would shoot their loads watching me shoot mine.

For similar reasons, I enjoy going to massage parlors. I enjoy meeting these pretty young girls for the first time, getting naked with them and having them stroke me all over. Of course, it's especially great when they get to stroking my cock, and I always watch the process intently. I love the complete nakedness and exhibitionism of the massage and love it when they concentrate on my cock and watch me orgasm and ejaculate.

About a year ago, after the masseuse had stroked my penis to erection, I plucked up the courage to take over from her and stroked myself to a h-u-g-e come with her there, naked and watching me.

A couple of months later, I went to a fairly up-market brothel, stripped naked in front of this very pretty, very naked total stranger, played with my cock, stroked myself hard and then masturbated to orgasm without her touching me at all. I generate lots of pre-come when I do this and get pretty excited. And when I ejaculate it is always a good shot, rather than a dribble.

I once had a double massage. It was fantastic! Two naked girls with me, one stroking my cock, the other tickling my balls and both of them watching me come.

A certain amount of exhibitionism is involved, but it seems to be that "Lyle" is really searching for someone to provide acceptance and permission for him to go ahead and take pleasure in masturbation. By getting masturbation out of the darkness and presenting it to his fantasy partners and prostitutes, "Lyle" is celebrating the act as something he's not ashamed of.

The Uses of Adversity

Another fantasy, from "Casey," who lives in Galveston, Texas, includes a preface that puts masturbation into a totally different context:

> My biggest fantasies revolve around masturbation. The thing is, I don't come easily. I need a lot of stimulation and nowadays with safe sex and condoms I seldom ever have enough sensation to reach orgasm while making love. Every cloud has its silver lining, I guess: It's made me a much more attentive lover. Knowing that I'm not going to get off during the act makes me concentrate my full attention on my lover's pleasure. The whole point of it is her orgasm. My own is deferred until after, at which time my lover may masturbate me or, if she's tired, I'll jerk off while she watches or plays with my balls.
>
> My fantasies started changing because of this. I used to have what I'd guess are fairly standard fantasies. I'd imagine seducing a woman I saw day to day, I'd watch her strip or undress her, explore her body with my fingers, tongue and lips, slowly exciting her until she was warm and moist and eager for my cock.
>
> Once I started having trouble coming inside a woman—numb through the rubber—I couldn't get too excited about the thought of just fucking. Instead, I started incorporating the real-life element of jerking off.

• • •

The message here from "Casey"—and it is an important one—is that masturbation is not deviant, kinky or something to be ashamed of and outgrown. He is using it as a perfectly legitimate technique to achieve sexual satisfaction that would otherwise be unattainable.

"Casey's" fantasy continues:

> *In* one fantasy, I'm an exhibit in a class made up of young female sexual research students. The subject is male masturbation, naturally. There's an older woman, in her early forties, who whips back a curtain and there I am, naked and lying on an examination table. I lie quietly, hands at my sides, as the lecturer instructs the class to watch me closely. I see the young women grow flustered. Some giggle, others lean forward intently, some cross their legs tightly and rock a little, obviously titillated by seeing me exposed like that. There's a buzz of conversation and the lecturer tells them to be quiet and watch. She walks to my side and begins to lightly fondle me, her manner clinical and matter-of-fact, explaining to the class that most men need visual or tactile stimuli to arouse them.
>
> Under her cool hands, I begin to grow. My penis grows out straight and stiff, jutting up and jerking with each beat of my heart. The lecturer steps back and takes a seat in the front row as I begin stroking myself.
>
> There are many variations. Sometimes, I simply jerk off as they all watch me. More commonly, there's some sort of audience participation. Sometimes it's a small room where women stand clustered around the exam table, observing each stage of my excitement at close range, lightly palpitating my testicles to feel them tighten as I'm ready to shoot, brushing my nipples when they've grown hard, spreading

my legs to expose my genitals fully, handling me freely as they choose.

Sometimes an audience member serves as my visual stimulation, baring her breasts to me, or sliding her panties down under her skirt and raising the front so that I can see her pubic hairs and lips. When I come, the young women cry out as they see my semen spurting across my belly and thighs. Afterward, I answer audience questions about what I felt and thought, and usually I am so aroused by this that I'm ready to come again, and the lecturer lets the audience choose if they wish to see another demonstration.

A similar scenario takes place in another audience setting. This time, the young women are members of a sorority. I'm a fraternity pledge who, as part of my hazing, has to submit to following their directions as I jerk off on command. They laugh and comment, telling me to stop and start, keeping me trembling on the verge of orgasm for hours. The scene gets them so excited that they masturbate; I watch them writhe in ecstasy nearby, lying on cushions or couches near enough to touch as they tease themselves with vibrators and stare at my engorged manhood. Sometimes they get so turned on that I'm ordered to lick them to orgasm or lightly caress them while they masturbate. When they are satisfied I'm ordered to shoot off.

I haven't really given this a lot of thought, but groups seem to be a part of many of my fantasies. The strangest—and perhaps most exciting—is something even more impossible than the first two. In this one, somehow I have a number of young beautiful women who are lying on a large bed, naked. I lie on top of them; their fingers brush me and touch me all over. They lick and kiss and nip me with their teeth, and I stroke myself while reaching out to fondle their breasts or run my free hand over their pussies. I lie on a warm, wriggling blanket of flesh and jerk myself off, shooting over their smooth bodies as they whisper encouragement and squirm excitedly.

My lover doesn't know about my fantasies, I'd be embarrassed to tell her. Maybe she'll read them in the book. I'd be very interested in her reaction. It would be pretty exciting to me if she thought they were sexy.

"Casey" has a secret that he is willing to share only with fantasy women. I suspect he's not much different from millions of other men who masturbate secretly, all the while longing to be "caught"—even indirectly, as "Casey" suggests, by having his lover read about his scenarios in a book.

An Exciting Hobby

This final masturbation fantasy, from "Dale," who is twenty-seven and manages an auto-detailing shop in the Chicago suburbs, also features a theme of discovery. In his case punishment is involved.

I find the "naughtiness" of masturbation very exciting. I like to imagine myself as a naughty boy who just can't help playing with himself (not too far from the truth, actually). The women of my fantasies either watch me with scornful amusement, or attempt to punish me for my wickedness. I have masochistic/submissive tendencies and frequently fantasize about a domineering nurse or governess who catches me playing with myself and tries to cure me of my masturbation habit.

Some of the more complicated fantasies I have acted out with my wife. When I feel that I need "corrective discipline," I go to her humbly and confess my naughty acts. She lectures me sternly on the evils of giving in to my habit, and proceeds to lower my britches and stretches me across her lap. She spanks my naked bottom, scolding me all the while. I beg for her to stop, crying, promising to be good, kicking my legs, and rubbing my penis against her legs until finally my semen squirts all over her lap.

Other times she plays a nurse who administers a sexual therapy treatment to control my masturbation habit. She ties me kneeling across a chair on my hands and knees, with my legs bound well apart. She takes my penis and begins slowly milking me as if I were a cow. She stops whenever I grow too near to climax, to teach me "self-discipline." If I grow too excited, she slaps my testicles and penis a few times. She keeps this up until I am begging and pleading with her for permission to ejaculate, but only after I've given her a humiliatingly detailed account of my recent masturbation activities.

I spend untold hours at my hobby of masturbation, and for several years now, I have been writing out my fantasies even as I play with myself. The mechanics are somewhat challenging, as I sit with pen in one hand and baby-oiled penis in the other. But the literary effort is extremely rewarding because it allows me to focus on and concentrate on the fantasy for hours at a time, resulting in some remarkably good ejaculations.

None of the masturbation fantasies that I've seen involve a man simply masturbating by himself. That suggests to me there is a desire to end the isolation and return to a sharing of sexual pleasure. It's that male cause-and-effect thing again. Our sexual role is to provide pleasure to our partner. When we fail at it—or think we're failing—there's trouble, a whole lot of complicated trouble.

Many men think they are cheating their wives or girlfriends when they masturbate. They develop elaborate ruses to protect their secret and if caught at it are deeply embarrassed. To complicate the situation, women don't have a book of etiquette to rely on when and if they discover a husband or boyfriend masturbating. It's usually something your mother didn't tell you about.

So I'll tell you.

What's important is to realize that masturbation is usually not a threat to a relationship or a sign that something is lacking. Men masturbate for all of the reasons that I've already discussed—the most important of which is that it feels good. The furtiveness associated with masturbation can be easily confused with an indication that hidden motives are involved.

Don't jump to conclusions. The chances are excellent that it has nothing to do with your relationship as a couple, and everything to do with his special relationship—an even older one—with his right hand (left for southpaws).

I know, I know: Why does he masturbate if he is sexually satisfied? A logical question. Again, go back and review the reasons I've already cited in this chapter. And remember, too, that sexual arousal doesn't just occur in bed or somewhere else where a couple can seek immediate fulfillment. I've seen estimates that men have erections on the average of every ten minutes. These sexual tickles accumulate to a powerful itch that men scratch by masturbating.

Can't it wait? Sure. But why wait? Masturbation does not adversely affect sexual performance or interest. On the contrary, sex therapists counsel men who have problems with premature ejaculation to use masturbation techniques to enhance their ability to time orgasm. For that matter, masturbation is one of the oldest self-taught methods for dealing with acute states of sexual arousal and nervousness, such as the first time with a new lover, which can bring on ejaculation almost immediately after penetration. A man will excuse himself, masturbate and then return to resume lovemaking.

. . .

Masturbation really doesn't need any warning labels. It is, however, habit-forming. Not addictive—habit-forming. Like all human pleasures, masturbation reinforces the tendency to return again and again to the source of the enjoyment. There's no physiological or chemical dependence, as there is with alcohol or drug abuse, but most of us can't resist giving a pleasurable experience an encore or two—or three, or four.

In the last fantasy, "Dale" seems habituated to masturbation and if he is spending "hours" masturbating, I'd say he may have gone beyond a habit to an obsession. Any activity, fantasy or real, that "takes over" to dominate our lives—an eating disorder is another nonsexual example—is a danger signal. The distinction I am trying to make is that masturbation, even habitual masturbation, is not the same as *compulsive* masturbation. Any sexual act that becomes compulsive does threaten a complete and satisfying sex life. If I stop going to work so that I can spend the day watching X-rated movies in Times Square, I've become compulsive. Compulsive behavior crowds out most everything else. It is an irresistible impulse to perform an irrational act. Going to see X-rated films is not irrational, nor is masturbation. What's irrational is the impulse to sacrifice a job, a family life or other aspects of one's sexuality for a short-term erotic high.

What I'm saying is that masturbation that excludes all other sexual options isn't just another kinky example of the joys of freedom of choice in twentieth-century America—there's a problem.

But most habits stop short of obsession, and the masturbation habit, it seems, takes hold first in adolescence when the sex drive is approaching its peak. There simply aren't enough sexual partners readily available to most young guys when the raging hormones are at full cry. Masturbation becomes a substitute for sexual intercourse, and it's a good thing. Our high schools and junior highs are chaotic enough. Without the release of sexual tension provided by masturbation, fourteen- to eighteen-year-old males would be even more distracted and difficult to teach than they are already.

This may explain why male genitals are exposed and easily manipulated: a built-in male pacifier. Mother Nature knew that sexual partners would be in short supply from time to time and made alternative arrangements in the interest of social harmony and to protect all creatures great and small. Some medical researchers also believe that constant production of new male sperm by masturbation or frequent sexual activity may be linked to the sperm's vigor and viability, and therefore promotes increased fertility.

The pluses probably outweigh the minuses, but there is one downside to adolescent masturbation. Putting a premium on coming quickly, particularly to avoid detection, can lead to a loss of control that leads to premature ejaculation during intercourse.

If adolescence is where the habit starts—the bad habit of using masturbation as a quick and easy release from sexual tension—there's no reason that it has to last a lifetime. As far as I'm concerned, women are the key to making masturbation a regular part of the mainstream sexual repertoire.

I'd say that most men have learned more about good sex from women than the other way around (women learning from men). Women have been in the forefront of thinking and talking about sex for the last thirty years, and as a result men have been exposed directly and indirectly to their own shortcomings as lovers and to ideas they never previously considered.

When I was promoting my first book on the talk show circuit a few years ago, I watched another author score a home run when she compared the typical male notion of foreplay to tuning an old TV set. To illustrate the point she held up both hands at breast height, tweaked the "knobs" back and forth and then dropped them to crotch level and twitched her fingers a little. The audience, mostly women, howled with laughter.

That was a terrific lesson for every man who was watching.

Through a bit of lighthearted teasing, we were being encouraged and given permission to be more creative with our foreplay techniques.

The same sort of permission needs to be given when it comes to masturbation. And I think it is slowly beginning to happen.

Books and articles about female masturbation in recent years have helped take some of the edge off the male masturbation taboo. In many ways it is a form of permission. And the next step? Consider this: Talk about it and suggest that he masturbate in front of you. Many couples enjoy mutual masturbation as a part of their lovemaking routine. It's one of many pleasurable techniques. It beats being petted and fondled like an ancient Magnavox.

But a mutual conspiracy of silence about masturbation isn't going to do either sex a service. My interviews and questionnaires kept turning up comments that suggested there is a deep reluctance on the part of many men to raise the subject. This diffidence is amazing given our ability to communicate the desire for oral or vaginal sex. No problem there!

But masturbation is a problem. It is one sex act that we have real ambivalent feelings about. Several men have told me that after years of agonizing about it they finally mentioned it to their wives but were rebuffed. Clearly, if women bring the same uneasiness about masturbation into the bedroom there's little chance of a resolution.

It's important to recognize that in general masturbation is not a threat to women. As powerful a pleasure as it is, masturbation will *never* totally replace sex with another consenting adult.

And while I've learned never to say never, on this one—never!

Part IV

Other Options

Twelve

Secrets of Power, Pleasure and Pain: Bondage and Spanking

Not long ago the Marquis de Sade was a very, very dirty old man—about as filthy as a toilet seat in a Grand Central Station public lavatory. Today, de Sade—or his bag of tricks—is awesome, like you know, a yuppie boomer in a *Beemer* or a Gen-Xer boogying on Wenceslas Square.

S&M is trendy. Hot. It has an edge. And it appears to be working its way into the sexual repertoires of consenting adults who at one time considered the occasional dominance and submission role reversal—I'm thinking of Linda on top and Larry on the bottom—to be pretty daring, dangerous stuff.

Welcome to the 1990s, where the well-dressed young man wears an Armani dog collar and a leash. Ladies who still lunch do so in leather and chains.

One way I keep track of sexual trends is through the mail we get at CNBC's *Real Personal*—bags full of comments and suggestions for shows. Before I started hosting *Real Personal* I would have guessed that one out of fifteen or twenty correspondents might ask us to do something with S&M. Actually, it's closer to three or four out of ten.

There's a lot of interest in the subject, and I suspect it's not just of an academic variety. One indication is that S&M imagery has been showing up all over TV, movies and fashion ads. Madonna caught the wave a few years ago with her video and best seller, *Sex*. Fashion designer Gianni Versace gave his clients a thrill in 1992 with the bondage look.

If Madison Avenue is seeing whips and chains on the radarscope, we'll soon be able to buy them in bulk at the Price Club and WalMart. American business has always specialized in selling what sells. And—surprise!—sex sells. But this time we're peddling a sexual taboo. That's new, that's different. It may even be progress.

There's nothing like a direct question. When I ask men, "Are you into S&M?" I get interesting answers. Not necessarily articulate ones, but revealing from a body language standpoint: shrugs, head waggling, raised eyebrows, chewed lips and a variety of itches that need scratching.

For something that is so *sooo*—this wave, next wave and the wave thereafter—there's a puzzling lack of resonance. Occasionally I'm treated to a graphic adventure involving penis piercing or what have you, but mostly S&M seems to be admired from a distance.

However, when I ask, "Do you ever pin your partner's hands to her sides or to the bed when you make love?" the response is very different: "Sure. A lot. She likes it and I do too."

Ah! I think I understand a little of what's happening. It suggests that "vanilla sex," a term the exotic erotic crowd uses to describe mainstream, non-cutting-edge sex, is evolving toward an acceptance of S&M from a starting point that's probably best labeled "Vanilla Plus." Decaf S&M.

Pinning your lover's arms to the bed amounts to bondage lite. It's the place where S&M starts. Easy, innocent, pleasurable.

But there's nothing new about that. Adam probably did it to Eve, and vice versa. What's new is the willingness to let bondage take its natural course, from pinning the hands to using the sash of a robe, to silk scarves, to ropes, to handcuffs, to who knows what and where.

Bondage is the threshold to the world of S&M, and many people don't even know it. Like the guys above, they're shocked if you tell me they are practitioners of S&M. Shocked and thrilled.

I think the thrill comes from enjoying a mild form of outlaw sex while knowing that there's no harm done. Pain is not necessarily a part of bondage—nor some other forms of S&M, for that matter. On the surface, it's all about dominance and submission.

And the thing is dominance and submission are no strangers to vanilla sex. Who's on top, him or her? Who initiates sex? Who refuses? Good questions. Yet, there was a time—and not long ago—when those questions simply were not asked. Not aloud, anyway. The rules of sexual etiquette were strict: Men dominated, women submitted.

Fortunately, things changed. Whatever the reason—women in the workplace, the Pill, the Bomb, Elvis, fluoride in the drinking water— there was a bedroom revolution that altered the dominance and submission status quo. Little by little, women moved toward erotic equality.

When that happened a whole range of sexual taboos, including S&M, were certain to be reevaluated. But of course! If Judy gets a thrill out of initiating sex, instead of waiting passively for her boyfriend to make the first move, what other aspects of dominance will appeal to her?

Let the experiments begin. And they did.

Bondage was and is the logical place to start. In male fantasy scenarios, it is only logical that forms of bondage would show up as a popular feature. The plot lines at this stage tend to walk on the mild side.

Wheel Personal

This is "Tom's" fantasy. He told me: "I'm a thirty-three-old manufacturing manager, living in White Bear Lake, Minnesota. My significant other and I have been together for several years. We enjoy each other's company emotionally and physically . . . but are not yet ready to take that final plunge."

My usual fantasy is actually half fantasy/half reality. Some of it is true but there are parts of it I have expanded on. If I knew back then what I do now, it would have happened this way.

I was dating this girl in high school and one night we took a drive out to Make Out Point—a little hill overlooking a pond where you would park your car and revel in the night. We started to kiss and she was looking at me quite seductively. She took a piece of rope out of her pocket and said, "Tie me to the steering wheel," in an extremely authoritative voice. I obeyed. I took her arms and pinned them behind her and attached the rope from underneath and eventually around the steering wheel. "Now recline the seat as far as it goes and come and sit in front of me."

I pushed the seat all the way back and sat in front of her while her legs straddled around me. "Touch," she whispered in my ear. I took my hand and slid it up into her dress and into her panties. My fingers were swimming in her wetness and she began to squirm around in enjoyment. I took my fingers out and tasted her. So sweet she was. I moved my head under her dress, kissing her thighs on my way up. I began to taste her, lick her . . . I wanted to be in her so badly . . . as I moved my tongue around inside her, I rubbed my hard-on at the same time . . . I longed for her but she was enjoying herself way too much for me to deny her.

I kept on eating her juices, until her body moved in wave-like motions. After she let out a long sigh, I undid my fly and penetrated. I wanted her to touch me but she couldn't. Her hands had not even explored my body for a moment. But this is what she had wanted. It was moving in and out of her . . . longing for her touch.

I untied her and she pounced on top of me, stroking my penis. She lowered her mouth and took me all the way. As I leaned back in enjoyment, she moved up my body and sat down on me. She started to rock back and forth, bouncing her huge breasts in my face. I licked them every time they slapped me, which made her even more aggressive.

When I finally came to the brink, I pulled her hips toward me in such a motion that our bodies merged into one and I came like never before.

"Tom's" girlfriend initiates the action but puts him in control. That certainly seems like a compromise to me. The bondage is voluntary on her part, sparing him the risk of being rejected if he had suggested the idea in the first place. Most important, as a couple, sexual power is being shared. It's her game plan, yet he is not threatened or deprived of the dominant role, which he appears to need and enjoy.

In turn, her desire to be dominated is balanced by the security of knowing that "Tom" is following her lead. They both give up something; both get something. Both win.

Complete Opposites

In this next fantasy, "Clay" and his lover are not sharing power. But they are sharing pleasure.

My fantasies encompass three different natures of love-making. The first is along the lines of unbridled passion. When you are hopelessly in love with someone and you are not concerned with anything but making love, you completely let go and let it happen. In this form of fantasy, sex is secondary to lovemaking.

The second fantasy type is when your partner does absolutely nothing except lie back and enjoy the entire sexual act. One partner is completely passive and vulnerable while the other one is completely dominant.

And the third of my fantasies represents most sexual encounters: the "I'll do this to you and you do this to me."

Well, let me get into more detail, namely with the second type. My partner lies on the bed naked. I proceed to tie her hands to the bedpost so that I can control everything and she can't partake in initiating any of the action. I move my tongue down her body, barely touching her and burning her with my breath. I put my tongue inside her and taste her wetness. She begins to moan and begs me to put myself inside her.

I tease her by flickering my tongue and kissing her thighs and the area around her belly button. I move up and begin to kiss her while at the same time I manually stimulate her clitoris with my fingers. She arches her back and I slowly pull my fingers out until they are just barely stimulating her.

I move away from her and begin to undress myself. As I slide my boxers down, my erection pops straight up. I want to put myself inside her so badly but I want her to wait it out. I start to touch myself . . . stroking myself up and down. I begin to rub against her body, rubbing my hard-on against her flesh. She is squirming underneath me, begging for me to enter her. After consistently rubbing against her flesh, I unwittingly penetrate her by rubbing my hard-on against her thighs. My penis slides right in on its own and I can't bear to pull it out. Her breasts are bouncing against my cheeks, and I grab her ass and pull her toward me.

She is moaning like crazy and the rope around her wrists keeps restraining her, pulling her back toward the bedpost. I pull myself out of her and start driving my penis in between her breasts. She pulls her head up to lick the tip every time it approaches her face. I get up and drop myself down her throat. She is taking all of me in. I get so stiff in her mouth, but I really need her tight wetness. I move down her body and put myself in and we bring ourselves to simultaneous orgasm.

There is a complicity between the partners in these bondage fantasies that serves to temper the control exercised by the men. He dominates the action but with "permission." In the case of "Clay," the fantasy picks up at a point where it is impossible to determine who initiated the action, yet it is clear that both lovers are enjoying the consequences equally.

Home Alone

"Bart" is thirty-five. He lives in Portland, Oregon, where he works at a nationally known air courier service. Here's what he told me about this fantasy:"I haven't had this fantasy for years, but it was numero uno when I was a teenager, and since then I've had no interest in bondage or S&M."

When my parents went out on a Saturday night, I'd take all my clothes off and walk around the house for a while. After about an hour, the thrill would wear off and I would go get some rope from the basement and tie myself up. I'd roll around on the floor trying to "escape," working myself up into a high state of excitement.

Usually, I'd fantasize that I was the victim of robbers who forced me at gunpoint to remove my clothes. They are two guys. One of 'em has a gun and orders me to jerk off. When they leave, I have enough slack in the ropes to get to the phone and call my girlfriend to come over and cut me loose.

When she arrives, she finds me naked, lying on the floor. She just sits on an arm of the chair in the living room and admires me. She takes pity—but instead of releasing me she rubs my body all over, takes my penis in her hand and slowly strokes it until I come.

An alternative to this fantasy was almost the same scenario but that my girlfriend and I were together when the robbers struck, they strip and tie us both up. I get loose first but instead of untying her, I explore her body with my hands and tongue.

If "Clay" had permission, "Bart" has an excuse. As a teenager he is looking for a way to justify his sexuality and the bonds, inflicted on him by the robbers, in this fantasy, help him come to terms with his strong, and probably, at that age, disturbing desire for erotic pleasure. He's not out to either take or relinquish power per se, it's the pleasure that motivates his action.

The Bonds of Marriage

I regard bondage fantasies as the frontier between two broad swaths of erotic territory that in the past rarely had much cross-border traffic. Now, however, travelers do go back and forth after having been introduced to the harmless pleasure of the lightest of S&M lite.

In this contribution, "Sal" illustrates how the process works. It's not really fantasy but a report on how one man's sex life has evolved from the starting point of bondage. He told me that his wife has made all the difference.

> *Her* tolerance has kept me sane and (more or less) faithful through twelve years of marriage.* She knows and approves of my occasional excursions to nude modeling studios, and I tell her of my experiences. . . .
>
> As for my interest in S&M: It began quite a long time ago. I can even trace the desire for bondage back to when I was five! During my teens and early college years, desires for normal coupling pushed out any S&M tendencies, and I was not even aware of noncustomary interests, except for my persistent practice of masturbation.
>
> After a few years of marriage, however, my hidden dimensions began to surface. More and more my fantasies centered on large-breasted dominant women who (for example) would tie me up and masturbate me with excruciating slowness, or spank me for abusing myself. I began collecting a number of "big breast" magazines, which lent themselves to my fantasies and private viewing. My wife was aware of my fondness for big breasts and self-abuse, but not of the rest of my fantasies. Nor did I play with myself in her presence.
>
> I began to experiment (still privately) with bondage, discovering a number of ways to tie myself up and act out my fantasies alone. I always made sure that my wife was absent from the home during these sessions, because part of the

---

*Don't ask! I have no idea how someone can be "more or less" faithful. I'm just passing along "Sal's" fantasy.

rapture of bondage is speaking and crying out aloud my most secret thoughts. The bonds on my flesh somehow liberate my spirit.

I would tie myself into a kneeling position in a chair and slowly bring myself to climax by pressing my genitals against the chair or with my penis inserted into a rubber masturbation tube . . . or bind a leather belt about my organs, securing the other end to the chair, and struggle in that tender trap until I spent my virility, with images of cruel female interrogators binding and torturing my sensitive genitals.

After a while I began timidly expressing some of my interests to my wife. She accepted them so readily that soon I was masturbating in front of her and receiving playful spankings on her lap. Later, after we read *The Joy of Sex* together, I articulated more of my bondage fantasies and we began acting them out.

There's more to this account than just bondage and submission to domination. I can see a deepening of the couple's relationship as he begins to share his fantasies and sexual secrets with her (reading *The Joy of Sex together* was an excellent idea). At first he's very wary but as he opens up and sees that she isn't rejecting him they move toward higher levels of fulfillment and satisfaction.

Let me digress for a moment from S&M to return to an important issue: communication. It's almost a religion for me. If men and women aren't willing to take the risks of communicating—and it can be scary and threatening—they are headed inevitably for conflict. Put it all on the table and talk. If there are irreconcilable differences it's better to know it now than to kid yourself for months or years.

The couple above could have gone for years pretending that "Sal" was just into "big breasts." But he "timidly," at first, expressed his other interests. I'm sure it wasn't easy. It was probably terrifying. But he did it—and what happened? She "accepted them so readily."

Find out where *he's* coming from. Find out where *she's* coming from. Find out where you're *both* coming from. Don't guess. Don't close your eyes.

Back to bondage. Actually back to spanking, which "Sal" mentioned in conjunction with being punished for masturbating. Of all those degrees of separation between "vanilla sex" and what *New York* magazine, in a recent cover story on S&M, called "mean sex," spanking is the one that introduces eroticism to the concept of pain as pleasure. It's just the beginning, though. While there is pain involved, the next three fantasies stop well short of "mean sex."

A Paddle for the Teacher

"Sandy" is an actor who lives and works in Toronto, Canada. He is twenty-four, married with one child, a boy, and aspires to work on Broadway. He told me, " I use fantasies in my theater work all the time. They help me define the characters I'm playing. Sometimes I have to think hard to remember which fantasies belong to me and which ones were generated by parts that I've played."

> *I* have several favorite spanking fantasies. The one that recurs the most involves a shy and demur schoolgirl who has been naughty. I'm her teacher and must dole out punishment.
>
> Usually, the scenario has the girl staying after school. The classroom is empty except for the two of us. I say, "What am I going to do about you?" She hangs her head in silence for a moment and then replies softly, "Spank me." I pretend to

be shocked, "You're a little old at fifteen for spanking." She blushes deeply.

I get up from behind the desk and remove my belt. "Okay. Spanking it is." I tell her to turn around and bend over. She obeys at once. "Pull up your skirt to the waist," I say. I hear her stifle a gasp. "Well, come on." She does as she's told, exposing a pair of pink striped panties. I keep her in that position while I lecture her on turning in her homework on time. Her knees tremble slightly. "I promise I will, sir," the girl says. Without another comment I carefully pull the panties down to her knees. "Are you ready?" I ask. "Yes, sir," she says meekly. I slap her bottom with the belt six times. At each stroke she moans deeply. When I finish I tell her to turn around and she does, still holding her skirt above her waist. "Are you sorry?" I ask. She nods. I gently pull up her panties, "You can go now."

The other variations on the theme are husband and naughty wife, the boss and his bungling secretary and the school principal and the prim librarian who must be punished for allowing her shelf of encyclopedias to get out of alphabetical order. I'm always the spanker in these fantasies. Sometimes, I turn the women over my knee and spank barehanded. Occasionally she gets down on her hands and knees. The women never resist me and have to be disciplined often for their infractions.

This is rather typical of spanking fantasies. Most of them involve punishment for misbehavior. I can't recall seeing one that came right out and said, "I like being spanked or spanking for the pure pleasure of the experience."

There's always a rationale and it suggests to me that spanking is a price that's being exacted or paid for sexual pleasure. Without it "Sandy" might feel guilty about actually enjoying his sexuality.

Nursing a Grievance

"Leroy" is forty-eight years old. He spent twenty years in the Air Force and now works at an aerospace company in Missouri.

I've never actually been spanked—as an adult, that is. But I do think about it, particularly when I'm away from home on business trips and spending nights in lonely hotel rooms.

My "script" stars a nurse who is furious with me for arriving late for an appointment with the doctor. She tells me to go into the examination room and take off my shirt and trousers. I do as I'm told. In a few minutes, as I'm standing there in my boxer shorts, the nurse comes through the door and closes it behind her with a crash. She scolds me for being late and lousing up the doctor's schedule. I attempt to apologize but she cuts me off.

"Turn around," she commands. I obey.

"Pull down your shorts." I begin to protest. "But I—"

"Quiet."

The nurse grabs the elastic waistband of the shorts and yanks them down. They fall around my ankles. I'm acutely embarrassed. "You'll have to learn your lesson," she says. "Bend over."

Again I try to object but she starts slapping my ass with a series of open-handed right and left hooks, like a boxer. I'm standing in front of a full-length mirror and can see her behind me swinging away. I can also see my cock getting hard. As she strikes, the nurse yells, "bad, bad." After about twenty slaps I come, firing sperm half way across the room.

The nurse stops hitting me and leaves the room. I quickly dress and get out of there. As I hurry through the waiting room, the nurse looks up from her desk, smiles and says, "Have a nice day."

One of these days an author should do an entire collection of nurse fantasies. I think it would be a marvelous tribute to the profession. Men have doctor fantasies but those are outnumbered by scenarios about nurses two or three to one. They are expressions of vulnerability put into the context of trust and a willing submission to a powerful, accomplished woman.

With a nurse, a man doesn't have to reluctantly give up his male roles—fussing, fretting and fighting all the way—circumstances, such as hospitalization or a physical exam, require it and he lets go.

The Customer Is Always Wrong

"Ned" is thirty years old, single and lives in Montgomery, Alabama. He is a technician in a medical lab.

In my best spanking fantasy I'm a woman trying on clothes in a department store dressing room. I'm there in a bra and panties and high heels. Suddenly, the curtain is pulled back. The store manager is standing there. He is pissed.

"You've been in here for an hour," he shouts, "and you wrinkled some of our best dresses," he adds. The next thing I know he has sat down in a chair that's in the corner and pulled me across his knee. "I've had it with this shit," he declares, and rips off my panties. He tosses them across the small cubicle. "Is this one of my bras?" he asks but before I can answer he rips that off too.

I'm still wearing the heels but otherwise I'm totally naked

and stretched over his knees. He spanks me hard for about ten minutes. When he stops, I roll off onto the floor, reach up, unfasten his belt, pull it clear of the loops, unbutton his pants and pull them down. "My turn," I say.

The manager dutifully turns around and kneels on the chair. I whip him with the belt while he masturbates. When it's over, I put on his clothes and he dresses in my frock and we go our separate ways.

Strange, eh?

"Ned's" fantasy involves cross-dressing and spanking. I wonder— there's really no way to tell short of psychoanalysis—if he's being punished for the thought of dressing up in women's clothes? It seems logical, but in this case, and in the other spanking fantasies, the discipline isn't severe enough to even provoke a comment about the attendant pain. There's a blurring of the pain and the pleasure.

I confess: I really have mixed feelings about this form of sex play and other varieties of S&M. It's good, it's bad, and it can be ugly.

First, the good. A few years ago, on *Real Personal,* we did a show that introduced the concept of "soft bondage." Ostensibly, it means that the paraphernalia isn't straight out of a medieval torture chamber. Hands may be tied with silk scarves rather than bound with chains.

Soft bondage also tends to be without pain. Loss of control and vulnerability provide the thrill. When I interview people about this form of bondage I'm struck by what has to be described as the innocence and romance of it all. I know it doesn't fit the S&M image. But both men and women say they get off on yielding to their partner's complete faith and trust, and in turn—on the dominant side—receiving that trust.

Imagine: You're stark naked, bound hand and foot. Nobody in his right mind voluntarily allows that to happen, unless he or she trusts the other person. And it's that rare gift that supercharges the atmosphere for both partners. I've heard it again and again: "Barry wouldn't hurt me," "Liz loves me and wouldn't dream of inflicting pain," "Tom constantly checks to make sure I'm all right." It's as if these lovers are demonstrating their commitment by brandishing potentially destructive power but not using it.

In many ways, some soft-bondage relationships are the strongest of any that I know of. The partners have confidence in one another. As in a circus high-wire or trapeze act, one partner willingly lets go and steps out into thin air knowing that the other will be there. Conversely, the dominant partner is stimulated by receiving this responsibility.

Sounds great, doesn't it? But this stuff isn't for everybody. That's what worries my about the trendiness of S&M. Most couples who are deeply into S&M, even if it is only soft bondage, take it very seriously because the risk is enormous.

You can get badly hurt. Being tied up by a stranger or by someone you "kind of" know is asking for serious trouble. It's thrilling, all right. Russian roulette is thrilling, too.

My advice is that if there is the slightest hint of coercion involved it's time to say good-bye. Get out of there. Every responsible person involved with S&M agrees. In doing research for this book, I have never encountered a guy who didn't assure me when he raised the subject of bondage or other aspects of S&M with a new girlfriend that there was no—none, nada, zip—pressure.

Fine. But I'm sure there are men who do apply pressure, simply because they are into domination and control, and when that happens all the red lights should be flashing and alarm bells ringing.

Example: Katie and Neil, who are married and enjoy soft bondage and occasional sex play with such harder toys as handcuffs and foot stocks, told me that they have code words and hand signals in case things get out of control. Katie said she's never had to use them but wouldn't dream of being bound without a safety mechanism. And you know what, originally it was Neil's idea. He's the dominant partner, and throughout his S&M sex life, including women before Katie ar-rived on the scene, he made sure that if he heard the words "red bal-loon," things came to an immediate halt.

Good idea. And here's another: Go slow. Most couples who are seri-ously into bondage started out with the soft stuff and gradually moved on, feeling their way, extending the comfort zone. Many of them de-cide that soft bondage is as far as they care to proceed into S&M terri-tory. Who's to say that they are being too timid and missing the fun?

Who? Nobody but those two people. It worries me that S&M's new-found chic will seduce people into what can be a rather violent and dis-turbing realm. But that's the ugly part of S&M, the subject, along with the *bad* S&M, of the next chapter.

Thirteen

Secrets of Loving Dangerously: Hard S&M

Let's invent a new form of sex. Don't worry, it won't be as hard a task as it might seem at first. We'll use a tried-and-true technique for creating anything new: If it's white, make it black; if it's round, make it square; if it's large, make it small.

The paradigm is one of opposites.

Sick of saying yes? Try no.

Bored by simplicity? Embrace complexity.

This formula can be used for creating new cars or new cultures. The 1956 DeSoto loses its gaudy fins and gleaming chrome and evolves into an ovoid, minimalist 1996 Camry; the New Deal becomes the Newt Deal.

Therefore, a new form of sex wouldn't be romantic and tender. We've been there, done that. Rough and raw are more like it. Kisses? Sharing? Pleasure? Hah! Kick 'em, stick 'em, and hurt 'em.

Silk is replaced by leather. Roses go the way of bullwhips.

What we're inventing then is S&M, which, the last time I checked with the Marquis de Sade, is at least a couple of hundred years old. But the oppositional dynamics are in play and that is comforting to those who want and need what the old forms of sex no longer seem to provide. From the eastbound lane, do a "180" and proceed west.

And that's probably what is going on with the interest in S&M these days. We're in a transitional period in which the old sexual functions are changing, but the new forms of sexuality haven't really taken a hard and fast shape. Form does follow function, after all. But I don't believe that S&M—hard bondage and pit bull dominance and submission—are the sexual forms of the twenty-first century.

Fortunately though, this is a book of fantasies, in which form and function may have *nothing* to do with reality. It's a good thing, too, because I'm off the hook.

As I said in the last chapter, S&M makes me uncomfortable. Not S&M lite, not soft bondage or spanking. I have trouble with the degradation and violence that assumes such a prominent place in the more outer-edge varieties of the S&M movement.

Some of it is role-playing: "Dungeons and Dragons" for adults seeking entertainment, thrills or transformational experiences. But some of it is brutally real and poses, I believe, a danger to those who don't understand where the costume party ends and the horror show begins.

As products of the imagination, the fantasies in this chapter do not differ in sum or substance from masturbatory fantasies, older-women fantasies and any of the other themes that we've examined. I'd be inconsistent in the extreme to suggest that the content of one fantasy is harmless and that another is not. A fantasy is a fantasy.

But . . .

I'd be irresponsible if I didn't post a warning sign where I honestly felt one is necessary. We all know that some fantasies get acted out—directly or indirectly. Throughout the book, I've tried to stay neutral on that subject. At times, I may have sounded as if I was indicating that acting out a particular fantasy would not be the end of the world. On the other hand, if you recall, I urged everyone to think twice about acting out group sex and ménage à trois fantasies. In this case, thinking twice isn't enough. Think a couple of dozen times and keep thinking.

I don't want anybody to get hurt. Some S&M fantasies, if acted out, are dangerous. Hence, I am posting a warning sign. It's not a no-trespassing sign; that's not my job. I'm a reporter and I take the responsibility of providing information very seriously. I won't hold anything back because you do *need to know.*

What you don't know *can* hurt you. It's the operating premise of this book and my career as an author and reporter. S&M has been outed; it is out of the dungeon and out of de Sade's drawing room and into the movies, best-selling novels, shop windows and the Internet. It may even be playing in a bedroom near you.

The following three fantasies offer revealing—and disturbing— glimpses into the S&M realm.

Across State Lines

"Jeremy," forty-six, owns a fast-food franchise in Shreveport, Louisiana. He says he and his wife have done some bondage and dominance and submission role-playing, but nothing like this scenario.

> *As* she awoke, she became aware of the sensation of movement. Yes, she was in a car, moving along at normal speed. She opened her eyes, or more correctly, tried. She was blindfolded.
>
> Instinctively, she tried to reach up for the blindfold only to discover that her hands were bound at her side. "She's waking, sir," a woman's voice said with a strange slur. "Good, I expected her to come around at about this time," a familiar voice replied.
>
> She tried to respond, but discovered that her mouth was clamped shut by some mechanical device. Using her lips and puffing out her cheeks, she discovered that it seemed to be

some metallic clamp that encircled her head and held her lower jaw pressed up against the upper jaw.

She paid attention to her surroundings with what senses she could use. By the scent of the car, it was Richard's, her husband's. Yes! It was his voice that had replied to the woman with the slur. So, Richard must have drugged her with some sedative and carried her to the car, with the aid of some mystery woman.

She was still in the stiffly boned corset in which she remembered being dressed. Every breath she took caused the tightly laced corset to squeeze her gently. Her full breasts were compressed into cups and threatened to overflow. She wiggled her legs and determined that they, too, were secured, probably with the hobbles that she had worn while making dinner. Was that last night or earlier tonight? Richard had brought home some wine. Hmmm . . . that must have been how he had given her the sedative.

"You can call me Sally," the woman's voice said. "Master Richard has told me much about you. He has asked me many questions about being a slave and he has learned much. I think you will enjoy his plans."

Master Richard? Slave? Plans? Her mind whirled at the numerous questions she wanted to ask Sally. But who was Sally, and how had she come to be in Richard's car, with her, on this strange adventure? That would all have to wait. She was unable to ask anything now.

Shortly the car made a turn and slowed. The bumps indicated that they were off a main road and either on a dirt roadway or in an alley of some sort. The car stopped and she sensed the driver's door opening. "We're here, Jim," Richard announced, "Glad to see you again." "Me too," said another man (was that Jim?). "Everything is ready. I'll help Sally bring her in."

Her? She wondered if that was how she would be referred to by everyone. And why was Richard allowing some strange man to handle her, let alone Sally? The car door nearest her opened and she felt strong hands lift her out of the seat. Behind her she heard chains rattling in a strange rhythm. Sally! She must be walking in chains!

She was very confused. Richard had never shown any patience for her interest in bondage, let alone expressed any interest himself. Try as she might to have him join her, master her, he ignored the invitations. As wonderful a man, husband, partner as he had been, he never willingly offered to be her master. Sure, she had tricked him a few times. Like slipping keys to her handcuffs into his wallet when he went out of town. Or the time she wore a locked chastity belt and hobbles to his manager's Christmas party. But each time he had been very upset with her "shenanigans," as he had referred to them.

But now was this the same Richard?

Jim carried her about thirty steps, apparently into a building of some sort. When he stopped she was lowered into a chair with arms and a footrest. It felt like a chair from a barber's shop, because Jim (?) was able to adjust the height and position the back so that she was lying almost flat on her back.

"OK, Sally," Jim said, "you may begin to prepare her." "Yes, Master Jim," came the reply from Sally. She felt new objects being attached to her wrists and ankles. These were apparently straps from the chair itself. Sally then removed the original straps and pulled the new ones tight. Now she felt that her arms were secured to the arms of the chair, and her legs, held at several points, were spread farther apart than her shoulders.

What is happening? she wondered. Why would Richard

allow strangers to do this and what is going to be done? She blushed, realizing that the corset did not fully cover her sex and that it was open for all three (is that the full count?) of them to see. Just that morning she had clipped the hair as short as possible, and in the light of the room it looked almost bare.

"You may continue as we discussed, Sally," Richard said. "Yes, Master Richard." She felt Sally touch her thighs and couldn't tell if it was intentional or just a passing touch. Sally's chains revealed her location, and she was moving behind her. Another strap of some sort was put over her head and pressed on her forehead, preventing any movement of her head. Suddenly, the blindfold was removed. The light, bright and directed at her from several directions, hurt her eyes. She closed them until they could adjust to the light.

Sally was moving again, now at the foot of the chair. She tried to glance at her, but was unable to keep her eyes open in the glare. All she could see was the outline of a figure. She felt Sally rubbing some lotion over her vulva and mons. It was cold and felt slippery. Sally's fingers touched her clit and she was jolted, as if struck by lightning. The sensation passed slowly, as Sally continued to rub the lotion.

Again she opened her eyes and she discovered a mirror on the ceiling. Since it was out of the direct light, it was easier for her to look into the mirror and watch the scene around her. It was like watching a movie.

A woman in a white silk corset was strapped to a barber chair. Her arms and legs were secured away from her body, while a large metal device was clamped on her head. At her left hand she recognized Richard, while on her right was a man she had never seen before. His head was shaved and there were many tattoos visible on his arms. This must be Jim. At the foot of the chair was a nude female shape. It had a bald head and revealed several tattoos on the back of her body. She was kneeling between the legs of the woman in the corset. Her ankles wore leather cuffs, connected to a foot or two of thick chain. This must be Sally.

Sally was still rubbing the lotion into her mons and around her pussy. It looked like a white moisturizer. Suddenly she realized it was shaving cream! What are they doing?

After working the lotion into a thick lather, Sally walked over to a low table out of the light and came back with a razor. Kneeling again, she quickly and expertly shaved her smooth. Sally was even able to avoid direct contact with her clit, but she knew that she was getting wet due to the scene in the mirror about her and the amount of attention Sally was giving to her pussy.

Using a damp cloth, Sally wiped up any remaining shaving cream and stood off to the side. "That was very well done, Sally," Jim said. "Thank you, Master Jim." What caused such a strange slur? she wondered. She couldn't see Sally's face, but could look down on her from the mirror. It appeared that she had a very nice figure, her breasts jutting proudly from her chest.

Jim now brought the table into the light. The sparkle of bright light on the stainless steel caught her eye. The table was laid out like a surgical instrument array. There were hemostats, forceps, needles of various types, and syringes full of various colored liquids. Several folded towels and sponges completed the inventory.

"Now," Jim was addressing her, "I must inform you that you are no longer in your home state. The rights of women to disobey their husbands are much different here than your experience would indicate. They have the right to be owned by their husbands, or masters, for as long as the master is pleased. Once you fail to pleasure your master, he may have you thrown out of his household. Master Richard feels you have been walking the line for a long time. But rather than losing the investment he has made in you over the years, he discussed with me the possibility of modifying your behavior. So I introduced him to Sally, who has worked with me for many years. Sally explained that I have made several modifications to her body that have made it easier for her to please me, while at the same time making my punishments more effective. Richard has decided to have these same modifications installed in you, as a last opportunity for you to please him. If you choose not to have these modifications, he will have no choice but to release you to whatever life you can find on the streets. So I now ask for your consent to have your master's bidding done."

She couldn't believe what Jim was saying. Modifications? Pleasing Master Richard? Of course she would please him. All she ever wanted to do was please him. But what was going to be done? Would he really throw her out if she refused?

"Decide!" Richard roared at her from the other side. Weakly, she nodded her consent. "Good, let's get this over with, Jim."

"Fine with me, Richard. Sally, you stand at her head and watch for any signs of shock. Richard, if you'll hand me instruments as I request them, we'll be done quickly."

She couldn't see exactly what was happening, since the angle the mirror provided was obstructed by Jim. He pulled a small chair into the gap between her legs and seated himself directly in front of her parted sex. She felt her face flush at the thought of him being there. Sally shuffled up and was in her line of sight. "Just relax," she said. What was that? At the X-sound a bright flash of metal gleamed in her mouth.

Is that what causes her slur? The X sounded like a K. She must have been born with some defect and now have a clip in her tongue.

Looking back at the mirror, she saw that Jim was holding a marking pen. He was wearing black Latex gloves, which were in sharp contrast to his white skin. She felt him touch her bald vulva. It was more sensitive in its new bare state, and she almost jumped at the touch. He seemed to be measuring something with his other hand and then marking on her skin with the marker.

She felt three marks on each of her outer labia. Then he reached to her clit and stroked it several times. Quickly she started panting at the sensation, and she knew her large clit was responding by poking forward from the hood that normally covered its length. Working quickly, Jim placed two additional marks, one of each side of the clit.

"Ready," Jim said. "Hand me one of the large forceps." Richard, who had put on gloves similar to the ones Jim wore, handed a large instrument to Jim. When had he learned about such things? Is this what Sally had taught him?

Jim clamped the forceps to her labia and asked for another, and another as soon as the second was clamped. In short order there were six clamps biting deeply into her labia. She would have been yelling at them to stop, but the other clamp held her mouth tightly shut.

"You'll notice that of the eight needles on the table, six are identical. Pass those to me one at a time as I request them, Richard." Six? Eight? Needles? She couldn't believe what was happening! And Richard a participant?

She watched in the mirror, remote and removed, almost as if what was happening was a movie or was happening to some other person. Richard handed Jim a large needle. It glistened in the bright light. Jim held it near the forceps, pressing a small piece of material on the other side. "Ready," he said. A sudden thrust of the needle had pierced her. "Next."

She watched, a fine layer of sweat developing over her entire body, as Jim quickly did the remaining five piercings. She felt like a pincushion. But behind the humiliation, the pain and the fear, she felt a tremendous turn-on. An orgasm, the power of which she had never felt before, was building deep inside her.

"Richard, unfold the top towel and hand me the first hardware set." In the mirror, Richard reached into the towel and removed a shiny brass padlock. Is this the "hardware"? she wondered. Jim opened the hasp and tested the mechanism with the key in the lock. Then he removed the forceps from the lowest two piercings. As he pulled the needle out of her left side, he slid the hasp of the lock into the hole left by the needle. Richard took the needle and placed it in the dish on the table. The right side was handled just as quickly. Then Jim pressed the lock closed. It clicked shut with a loud snap and the key was given to Richard.

Oh, no! What is this? Are these the modifications you are making to my body? What will happen to me?

In quick order, Jim was handed two more locks, of which one closed the middle two piercings and the other crossed the top of her pussy. Their total weight pulled at her labia, creating an intense sensation that was adding to her arousal.

"Done with her for now, let's do the other end," Jim said.

Sally shuffled to help Richard move the table, as Jim found a taller chair. When he was seated, Jim began to adjust the head clamp, opening it very slowly. She thought this was being removed and she'd have a chance to talk to

Richard. The pain in her labia was like fire, but it was continuing to act as a powerful turn-on.

Just as the clamp allowed her to slightly part her lips, Jim and Sally surprised her by inserting a flat metal plate into her mouth. The plate was then attached to the rest of the device, and as the clamp was lowered, it pulled her jaw down, forcing her mouth open further and further.

She tried to speak, but her tongue waved uselessly against her lower jaw, which was not responding to her attempts at speech. She was able to make strange guttural sounds in her throat, but no one could understand her.

Jim picked up one of the syringes on the table and injected the contents into her tongue. "There, that'll go to work in a few seconds. Don't be afraid, it will interrupt the nerve impulses in your tongue for about ten minutes. That will immobilize your tongue until we are through."

Through? Through with what? Her eyes showed the fear and concern that she couldn't tell them about. Jim looked at her and understood. "Sally, show her what we're going to do." Sally shuffled closer than before and opened her mouth.

She looked at Sally and now saw that the flash of metal she had spotted earlier was a piercing in her tongue. It was a barbell stud on the underside and the top section held a small metal ring, about one quarter inch in diameter. Now she understood why Sally spoke with a slur.

"Your mouth is slightly bigger than Sally's," Jim was saying, "so we will use a three-eighths ring. This will allow Master Richard to pass a chain through the ring and attach you to any object. It also makes a very effective gag."

She couldn't believe any of this was happening. What was Richard going to do with her?

"Let's test that tongue now." Jim poked at her tongue with a needle. She felt nothing, and even though she wanted to move it out of the way, her tongue no longer obeyed her. "Fine, looks like we're ready."

Richard handed over another large forceps and Jim quickly clamped her tongue about an inch back from the tip. She closed her eyes, not wanting to see the image in the mirror. She felt her tongue being pulled out as far as possible. A short delay as Jim adjusted the needle in his other hand. Then a searing sharp pain as the needle went clear through her tongue.

Tears welled up in her eyes. She couldn't hold them back and she cried as Jim and Richard affixed the metal post and ring into her tongue. "We'll let her rest a few minutes," Jim said. "Sally, bring out some sodas."

Sally returned with the sodas to find the room much quieter. Jim and Richard were watching her rapid breathing. She had recovered from crying, and was now back into a high state of excitement from all that had happened.

Jim and Richard drank their sodas slowly, watching for any signs of excessive pain or discomfort. "She seems to be taking it very well," Jim said.

"Yes," Richard said, "I expected her to, even if she wasn't prepared for it so suddenly. I'm ready for the last one as soon as you are."

"Fine," Jim answered.

As Jim positioned himself between her legs again, Richard whispered in her ear. "I'm doing this because I love you and think you really love me, too. I have much to learn, and I know you can teach me, about being a master. At the same time, you have to learn to be my slave. The locks are there to remind you that you belong to me, at all times and all places. Once the piercings have healed we will visit a jew-

eler I know and have them engraved with my name and address. That way you will always be returned to me. The post
and ring in your tongue are for my pleasure. Sally has offered to train you in how to use them, and I'm sure you will
learn rapidly.

"This last picture is my gift to you. It will be exclusively
for your pleasure. I think you will enjoy it."

With that, Richard moved away and joined Jim at her
other end. He said to Jim, "Jim, I've thought about what you
said, and I agree. I'll do this one myself."

"I thought you would," Jim replied. He stood up and
Richard sat in the chair between her legs.

"I marked the location already, just stroke her a few times
till enough has cleared the hood to make both marks visible."

Richard stroked her clit, and she moved again, the same
bright excitement from the time Sally had touched her.

"Here's the forceps. Clamp them on so both marks are
still visible," Jim said.

The forceps felt much colder on her clit than any of the
prior locations. She let out a loud, deep moan as the pressure
of the forceps bore down on her clit.

"Now, press the cork onto the left side, and push the needle through in one smooth motion."

Richard looked up at her reflection in the mirror. "I love
you," he said, and then pushed the needle through her clit.

The orgasm triggered by the needle was so intense she
had no idea what was happening around her. She couldn't
move very much, but she was seeing stars and the room
slowly spun around her. Sally pressed a cool cloth on her
face. The fresh feeling was a relief from the heat and sweat
she felt all over her body.

When she came down from her high, she looked in the

mirror and could see the sparkle of a thick ring, about one-half inch in diameter, attached to her clit.

Now her new life would begin, now that her master loved her and she was going to be his pleasure slave forever.

The Price

"Gordon" is thirty-three years old. He lives in Norfolk, Virginia, where he is a house painter.

"OK, slave," she says, "you can have a few minutes to yourself to sit quietly. I'm going to take a shower."

Say it! Ask her! says the voice in my head. Now's your chance!

No, I can't, I answer. She'll just give me another whipping and I'm already so sore . . .

Say it, dope, it tells me. She's leaving. Say it now!

"Er . . . Mistress?" My voice is tentative.

She turns around, gives me that look, and I almost chicken out. But now I have to say something. I take a deep breath.

"Mistress, do you need someone to scrub your back?"

I can see the cloud darken her face, and I know I have lost. But, wonder of wonders, it passes and is replaced by a hint of a smile. She cocks her head at me and just looks for a moment.

"You want to scrub my back, slave?"

"Yes, Ma'am," I reply in what I hope is my most humble and ingratiating tone.

"Very well, then. You wait here while I talk to Master Tom."

I sit in my usual spot on the floor, feeling the rough carpet against my naked bottom. My penis is starting to throb. I cannot believe what seems to be about to happen.

She returns with my master. "OK, slave, up with you, follow me."

I get up, my legs shaky, and stumble to follow her. Master Tom follows behind me. I notice as I pass that he is carrying the cane and strap, but mostly I notice her wonderful jeans-clad bottom, moving ahead of me. I have lusted after that bottom so many times. Now I am about to see it, unadorned. My penis is doing a dance, seeming to have a life of its own. I feel lightheaded.

Into the bathroom we trail, a short procession. I do not look back at Master Tom, but I can feel his presence behind me, tall and powerful. She draws back the shower curtain and gets into the tub, still fully clothed. Master Tom positions me a few feet short of the tub, and turns me to face it squarely.

"Legs apart, wide!" he says.

I move my legs as far apart as I can consistently with reasonable comfort. He kicks the inside of my right foot with his boot, and I respond by moving that leg even farther out. I can feel the muscles on the inside of my thigh straining. I can also feel my penis straining, trying to grow even larger. She turns to face me.

"OK, slave, this is what you wanted, but each piece is going to cost you. *Hands in front!* Ten with the cane, Master Tom."

He lays them on with gusto, timing them so that the sting from each is just beginning to fade when the next one lands. His aim is entirely too good, for it feels that each is hitting in the same spot, and in the same spot I have had many dozens of strokes already this weekend. I am screaming and begging, as usual, well before the tenth is given. This one is directly up between my legs, not so hard as the others, but quite enough to elicit a blood-curdling scream as I jump and pull my legs together.

"Legs apart!" he says, emphasizing the command with a most wicked stroke to the side of my right thigh. Once again, I move my feet apart as far as I can, and he moves them even further.

"Slave, that display of disobedience will not be repeated, do you understand? she says. "If you make any move to bring your legs together again for the duration of this little exercise, I will declare it over and you will be severely punished, bound if necessary so that you cannot further disobey."

"Yes, Ma'am," I whimper. "I'm sorry, Master Tom."

I am sniveling slightly, but beginning to get my breath back. She slowly unbuttons her shirt and pulls it open, revealing her bright red brassiere. I begin to breathe deeply. I have seen her shirtless before, but never so close and never with the promise of so much more. Half of each bra cup is sheer and on the right side I can see most of the nipple clearly. The shirt slides off her shoulders and arms. She tosses it aside and stands facing me with hands on hips.

"Well, slave, is it worth what it cost you?"

I hesitate, earning me an *"Answer your mistress!"* and another swat on the thigh from my master.

"Yes, Ma'am, I think so," I say softly, and I can see her expression darken. "I mean, *yes,* absolutely, definitely, no question."

"Watch it, slave. I'll let this one pass because I'm such a gentle soul, but don't try my patience further. . . . Are you ready now for the next step? What do you think, Master Tom, aren't my jeans worth at least twice as much as my shirt?"

"I would think at least twice, Mistress Lori," he says. "In fact, I think twenty-five would be a nice round number. Furthermore, I think you should have the pleasure of administering them yourself. Here."

He hands her the strap, as my heart sinks to the depths of my body. From in front! I know what that means, exactly, and I do not think I can endure a fraction of what is coming.

"Why thank you, Master Tom. And just to be sure that these pesky hands stay out of the way, why don't you cuff them off behind his back. Remember, slave, your feet are to stay exactly where they are on the floor. You bring those legs together even one inch and you will be very sorry."

He jerks my hands behind me and cuffs them together. He must have had the cuffs in his pocket—I didn't see them before. I expect him to remove his hands after I'm cuffed, but he keeps them on my wrists, exerting pressure on the small of my back to keep me from backing away.

She begins, and the stinging fire starts almost immediately. I feel as though my penis and my testicles have been dipped in boiling oil as the strap cuts into them, left to right and then right to left, backhand. By the fifth and sixth blows I'm howling with the pain. My body tries to bend to escape the torture, but Master Tom keeps his left fist in the small of my back. He wraps his other arm around my chest just below my throat. He pulls back with the latter and pushes with the former, so that my pelvis is forced upward and forward, making me even more vulnerable to the blows of my implacable mistress.

I am screaming and begging, trying to back out of this deal, wishing I had kept my mouth shut. She is laughing, and now and then directs a blow directly up between my legs to catch my unprotected testicles full force.

Somehow, it ends, and Master Tom relaxes his grip on my

body. I'm surprised to learn that I managed not to move my widespread feet. I am also surprised to find, when she strokes me gently a time or two with the strap, that my genitals are still attached to my body.

"The jeans, now. Watch carefully, slave, I certainly want you to get your whipping's worth." Looking directly into my eyes, she unzips her jeans and casually lowers them, stepping out first with her left foot and then her right. She is wearing red bikini briefs to match her bra, and I think I have gone to heaven. This is more of her skin than I have ever expected to see in my life, and here it is just inches away from me. I can just catch the swelling of her sex against the crotch of the panties. I am in even more pain than after the first round, but I am also more excited. My penis, which collapsed during the earlier onslaught, is beginning to swell again. She notices and laughs.

"I don't need to ask this time if it is worth it, slave," she says with a smile. "I can see the answer for myself."

I feel my face redden. I have been naked before this women for the last three days. She has seen me erect many times, and has twice watched me masturbate at her command. Why am I blushing now? It can only be that the connection between my excitement and her body has never been more blatant, and it is embarrassing even to me.

"Well, now, the last two items are a package deal," she says, suddenly almost businesslike. "You get them together for one hundred strokes, given at the same time from both Master Tom and me."

"Mistress . . ." I say, suddenly worried again. "Does that mean one hundred strokes from you and one hundred strokes from Master Tom, or fifty each—one hundred altogether?"

"Aha, clever slave!" she laughs. "I hadn't thought of one

hundred each. But it sounds good to me. What say you, Master Tom?"

"You know me, dearest," he says. I know him too, and I know exactly what he means.

"Tell you what, slave. If you can keep an accurate count, we'll stop at fifty each. If not, we'll stop when each of us thinks his or her count is at one hundred. Of course, if we lose count we'll just stop when we get tired—how's that?"

"Oh, Mistress, please, I really don't think I can take that many. Please, can we just stop this whole things right now, please." I'm beginning to cry.

"Beware of getting what you want," she says. Ready, Master Tom?"

"Ready."

And the torture begins. I try to keep count, but with the two of them, each with a separate rhythm, it is simply impossible, and after no more than a dozen or so I have given up, sobbing and begging and crying again. I am too exhausted to scream full voice as I have been doing, but now and then an especially wicked blow will elicit a howl. Occasionally, I lose my balance, and Master Tom has to steady me with a firm hand on my shoulder. Twice, they get into an alternating rhythm that has my pelvis moving forward and backward in reaction to their blows almost as if I were attempting some sort of copulation with an invisible partner. The blows are more spread out than before, with her concentrating on my nipples now and then, and him striking my thighs, arms, and now and then up between my legs, still widespread somehow.

Finally, it ends. I can barely stand, and my breath comes in great gasps. She smiles at me and, without a word, moves her hands behind her to unfasten her bra-strap. Then she moves her hands back and forth in front of her breasts, holding the bra cups in place while she withdraws one arm at a time from the shoulder straps.

"Well, little slave, is this what you've been waiting for for so long?" she says with a smile. I haven't the strength to answer. Suddenly, my vision blurs as Master Tom whips my glasses off my face. I open my mouth to protest, but before I can the world goes completely black, and I realize that he has blindfolded me. I have the briefest of memories just before the darkness of seeing her hands move out and up, and the red bra beginning to fall.

"Oh, Mistress, it's not fair," I wail.

"Not fair, slave? How could your mistress be unfair? You are to scrub my back for me, is that not so? What else was promised? Now, hush while I bathe everything else."

I settle into a gentle sobbing. Master Tom puts something into my cuffed hands—it must be her brassiere. I clasp it convulsively.

"Here's one more thing to keep you company while I bathe," she says, and I feel her tie something made of fabric under my scrotum and around my penis.

"Why look, Master Tom, the red is almost as pretty as the bow he wore for us when he arrived." He chuckles agreement. I hear the curtain pulled closed, and the water start to fall. Then the sounds of bathing. My breathing is coming more regularly now, and I'm beginning to think again. How can I scrub her back when my hands are cuffed behind me and I cannot see? Maybe they will at least uncuff my hands, and I can feel her skin under my fingertips.

The water stops.

"OK, slave, time to do your duty. Open your mouth."

Without thinking I obey, only to have a soapy bath cloth thrust into it. It tastes vile. Master Tom puts one big hand on each side of my head to guide my motions, and she apparently moves her back as required to scrub it against the cloth. It seems anticlimactic, to say the least. A few times, the tip of my nose or a cheek touches her wet skin, but the rest of the time it is simply uncomfortable. I struggle not to swallow the soapy saliva.

This too eventually ends, and the cloth is removed. I can hear her rinsing her back, and Master Tom holds a cup of water to my lips for me to rinse with. I cannot get quite all of the soapy taste out, but it is much better. The sound of falling water stops, I can hear the curtain drawn once more, and the faint sounds of her toweling off.

"Now, slave," she says, "for your relatively good behavior, I have a small treat for you. Get down on your knees—Master Tom will help you."

With a gasp of pain, I move my stiffened legs together and, relying on master's grip for balance, go down on my knees. He adjusts my posture until I am in a half-sitting position, my body leaning forward. Once again, he takes my head in his hands and holds it very still. First faintly, and then stronger, I feel a tickle on the tip of my nose. It feels like hair, soft and curly. There is the aroma of freshly washed skin, and a hint of something else. Back and forth, horizontally, the tuft moves across the tip of my nose.

"Do you know what that is, slave?" Her voice comes from above me. I do, but cannot speak. My penis is swelling again.

"He does," says Master Tom. She laughs with him as the tickling stops.

A few minutes later, I am sitting once again on the living-room floor, my blindfold and cuffs removed at last. I still have her panties tied around my penis and testicles. My bottom is not too bad, but my genitals are still quite sore. My mistress has dressed and sits with Master Tom in the lounge chairs opposite.

"Do you really feel cheated, slave boy?" she says. "Are you really dissatisfied?"

I take a deep breath. "No, Ma'am," I say softly. I am surprised to realize that I really mean it.

"In fact," she continues, "wouldn't you go through that same ordeal again, right now, with no reward at all? Isn't that what you really want?"

I begin sobbing again, softly, and then louder as the tears come to my eyes and I am helpless to stop them.

"Answer your mistress," says Master Tom, gently but firmly.

"Yes, Ma'am. Oh, please, yes, Ma'am." The tears are coming harder than ever now. They look at each other.

"Up, slave!" she says. I get to my feet to face her, and she briskly jerks the cloth from my crotch.

"We won't need this, will we?" she says. "It'll just be in the way."

"Spread your legs," Master Tom commands, with a laugh. *"Wider!"*

The Mountain Top

"David B." (to distinguish him from "David" in Chapter Two) is a twenty-nine-year-old college career counselor and administrator from the Midwest. I summarize the introduction to the scenario in the interest of length. His fantasy involves a private ski slope in the Alps that his girlfriend Sarah has told him about. It proves to be an enchanting place, remote and challenging, with deep, unbroken powder snow. He is alone there and notices a chair lift with only a single chair that could carry him to the top for another run. "David" climbs aboard, pushes a button, and the mechanism comes to life—but in an instant he finds himself bound to the chair by powerful clamps and blinded by a hood that unfurls down on him. The lift bears him upward toward a mysterious-looking chalet.

The journey seems to last for ages but eventually the noise of the rollers and the reduction in speed indicate that the chair is slowing down. As it comes to a silent stop the hood retracts from about my face and I am able to see for the first time. The chair has arrived in the middle of a large open-plan area in the middle of what I take to be the chalet on top of the mountain. The far wall contains a huge picture window, which looks onto the powder slopes that I had seen from below.

The room is massive and very expensively furnished. In one corner there is a life-size sculpture with the shape of a woman wrapped entirely in a silken material of many colors, leaving just the outline visible. My attention is quickly drawn back to the area in front of me as five beautiful ladies emerge from doors and alcoves on the other side of the room. They are all gorgeous and dressed in full-length mink coats and high heels.

I suspect that they aren't wearing much else under the furs, which is quickly confirmed as they open them to reveal creamy silk lingerie.

"Hello, David, I'm Fiona. We've been waiting for you." It is the girl in the center of the group who has spoken. She is clearly the leader, and speaks with a sexy French accent. "Ever since Sarah let slip that she had told you about our private ski slope we have been waiting for you to come. Sarah, as you can see, is paying for her indiscretion, and has been since yesterday afternoon." She looks toward the silk-swathed sculpture, held upright and rigid against its wooden support. Faint mewling sounds come from the figure.

The extent of Sarah's predicament becomes apparent a moment later as one of the girls speaks: "David, I'm very sorry that we haven't introduced ourselves yet. We are all members of the society of *Roissy,* a girls-only organization dedicated to the search for sexual fulfillment through bondage. Each year we take this chalet for the season and members bring their friends to introduce them to our particular pleasures.

"Every so often, however, a boyfriend, like you, or a husband finds out about our secret and we have to take action. We've recently developed a program that has proved very successful in teaching the males just who is the dominant partner in a relationship. Disclosure, of course, is not a practice we encourage. Sarah was particularly careless and has had to be disciplined. She has been immobilized like that for the last ten hours and has one more hour to go. The vibrator deep inside her is on a timer and switches on for fifteen minutes every half-hour. It is an exquisite torture but her punishment is not yet over, as you will find out later."

And indeed I do.

Another girl comes forward and blindfolds and gags me with a scarf. They move me out of the lift chair, trussing my legs and ankles with rope, binding my hands in front with scarves, lashing my elbows together and attaching the end to my ankle and knee restraints. The contortion is a painful one and not unlike the fetal position. They leave me fully clothed in my ski suit and encase me in a down sleeping bag, which is hoisted with a block and tackle to swing suspended beside the roaring fireplace.

My new friends say *adieu* as they retire for lunch. I dangle there for what seems like an eternity, becoming hotter and more sweaty by the moment. The suffocating heat, the painful bonds and the velvet hood that were draped over my face were unbearable. Just as I'm about to pass out, I feel the bag being lowered to the floor. Several hands work to release me from the sodden down cocoon, remove the cords and scarves, and strip off my sopping ski clothes.

I blink my eyes to accustom them to the light and take a deep breath of cool air. Over me stands a lovely creature. "David, I'm Mickey and I'm in charge of your indoctrination." She is completely nude and smiling. Despite the ordeal, my cock goes erect in reaction to Mickey's marvelous body. "Oh, no, Davy, that's not part of your indoctrination at all, certainly not for the next twenty-four hours. Susie, could you please fetch the cock restraint."

One of the other girls moves away and returns a moment later with a thick leather harness. The three of them force my legs through the holes in the harness, and Susie draws the apparatus around my waist and fastens it, flattening my prick between my legs, and then padlocks it behind my back. Mickey announces that it is time for my shower.

The girls frog-march me into the bathroom. My hands are still tied but no longer bound to my knees and ankles. This allows them to attach an overhead rope to my wrists and yank me upward onto my tiptoes. The pain is excruciating in my arms and gets worse as they attach a space bar between my ankles. An instant later, a cascade of freezing cold water streams down on me. I hear one of the girls say, "Five minutes of cold water will cool you down, Davy."

Five minutes! I figured to freeze to death in another thirty seconds. I'm shaking uncontrollably. Just as hypother-

mia begins to set in, the stream of water changes temperature. I stop shivering and catch my breath in the sudden,
blessed warmth.

Mickey steps into the shower with a sponge and soap. She
plants a lingering kiss on my lips as she begins to wash me.
The pain in my arms subsides enough for me to notice my
prick is straining against the harness.

She works gently and lovingly. As the last of the soapsuds
disappear down the drain, Mickey uses the towel to dry my
face, and then puts her arms around me and carefully licks
with her tongue the few remaining drops of water from my
eyelids, ears, nose and neck. She puckers her lips and blows
little puffs of air onto my skin and nuzzles me.

Despite the cock restraints and hanging by my arms, I
know I'm going to come. The urge is hammering down on
me like a freight train . . . and then she stops, steps back
from the shower stall and grins. "There, wasn't that nice?
No relief for you yet, Davy."

She and the other girls withdraw from the bathroom and
leave me hanging there. I must black out at this point because the next thing I know I'm in another room, on the
floor in the corner, with Mickey holding my head helping
me drink a cold bottle of Coke.

There's a vaulting horse in the center of the room, the
kind gymnasts use. A body is draped backward across the
horse and there are muted groans coming from the head of
the pommel. It is Sarah. She is spread-eagled across the device and her limbs are tied securely to each of the legs with
long blue scarves. A vibrator pokes from between her legs
and a second smaller one is visible in her rear passage. Her
head is swathed with multicolored silk, and she is gagged
and blindfolded.

A girl, who I haven't seen before, is massaging Sarah's breasts and clit, and is in the process of bringing her to an involuntary orgasm. "She is almost coming up to her second hour on the horse, Davy, and she's finding it quite tiring. Jane, on the other hand, is having a terrific time looking after her and finds it a real turn-on." Mickey says something about swapping my headgear for Sarah's. She was totally into her dominatrix role. The girls push and pull me toward the horse and I realize that there are still more torments to come.

The good, the bad, the ugly. You be the judge. Whatever the verdict, I'm convinced that the need to reinvent sex is at work deep in these fantasies. The old sexual forms aren't working for "Jeremy," "Gordon" and "David B.," so they are doing a "180" and traveling in the opposite direction.

It's a way to obliterate roles that are causing conflict and anxiety: Blast them out and replace them with others that are such powerful contrasts that they peremptorily silence any internal debate whatsoever. What bothers me, though, is exchanging one sexual role for another role that may be a lot less sexual than it is a dark and deeply misanthropic power trip (or its mirror image, a masochistic exercise).

Personally, I get jumpy when we start talking about sex and pain in the same sentence. Color me vanilla.

I'm willing to listen to people who say that the pain quickly becomes exquisite pleasure. Okay. It's just not something that turns me on. And what also does not turn me on is the idea of getting off by causing pain to someone else.

This is the aspect of S&M that can turn ugly and dangerous. I know, we're all big boys and girls and if we want to be hurt that's our constitutional right, just like not wearing a seat belt or riding a motorcycle without a helmet.

Excuse my sarcasm, but what concerns me is when S&M role-playing becomes revenge-taking. Sex is sex, not a way to get back at someone—real or symbolic, including yourself—for injustices that have been done. Sex that's used as a weapon is violence—not sex.

What I keep hearing about the harder forms of S&M is that they particularly offers women an opportunity to "top" men for a change and make up for a lifetime of being dominated and jerked around. As Shakespeare's King Lear said—"That way lies madness."

If that's the motive for dabbling in S&M, what you really need is a good assertiveness-training course, not a part-time job at the "Temple of Dom." Get a punching bag; take karate lessons. Cutting sex free from the tangled cultural, personal and emotional webs that have been woven around it is an admirable—and essential—objective. But the oppositional paradigm can be a false model.

We need a "sex positive" society, not one that uses sex to moralize, instruct, punish or take revenge. The harder forms of S&M have been in the "no-go zone" for so long that its adherents are rushing these days to repackage it in New Age wrapping. Fine.

Sell it as a form of hetero-drag, a walk on the wild side for bored suburbanites, a refreshing role reversal. Sell bad as good, pleasure as pain. Sell it as "safe sex"—nonpenetration sex—in the era of AIDS. Sell sadists and masochists as just another minority misunderstood or victimized by the straight, vanilla majority.

All I'm saying is—let the buyer beware.

Fourteen

Secrets of Cybersex:
From the Condom
to the Modem

I opened this book with the suggestion that there are forces at work to-day that could change sex as we know it. Fitting, isn't it, to conclude with a chapter that focuses on a process that is rapidly wiring up all our private parts and digitizing our desires?

The gods of unintended consequences were certainly chortling gleefully the moment the Internet started evolving into a twenty-four-hour-a-day global computer network for scientists and scholars. Of all the unforeseen possibilities, the very least of them was the creation of the first new medium for sexual expression and gratification invented since Buffalo Bob Smith asked "Hey, kids, what time is it?"*

Like television, the Internet is a mass medium (or quickly becoming one), and wherever people congregate, in prime time or real time, sex is quick to follow. But unlike television, cyberspace is two-way communication. It offers audience participation and, as a result, the content of *cybersex* is largely homegrown and homemade. This is an

---

*The Howdy Doody Show, circa 1951.

important development, in that erotica has traditionally been shaped by the producer, not the consumer, which acts as a mechanism to influence the subject matter in ways that may be at variance with otherwise prevailing taste.

What I'm saying is that for centuries those who wrote, drew, painted or photographed erotica did so to reflect and to promote their own sexual agendas. Unlike most people, they had the means to do so. To a large extent, their agendas became ours simply because they had access to the erotic medium as creators or distributors. Their books, postcards and etchings were printed and sold under the counter and along the Left Bank of the Seine. Now the medium is becoming accessible to anyone with a PC, a modem and a telephone line. You don't even need a beret or dirty raincoat.

Consequently, cyberspace is already functioning as an erotic bulletin board, open to all. Fantasies that once sprouted like mushrooms, but only in the darkness of one's imagination, are now easily transplanted to a public place.

Radio—and television, to a much larger extent—made porous the boundary between the public and private spheres of life. Electronic mass communication pried open closed worlds to ideas and behavior that wouldn't have been tolerated or imagined under other circumstances. Cyberspace does the same but goes a giant step farther by permitting the receivers to also act as transmitters. Suddenly, what you see, hear and get is no longer limited to that which is produced by a narrow segment of the population, those with the wherewithal to broadcast a message of self-interest, but expanded to all who are computer-literate (a term that just a few years ago meant educated, affluent and technologically adept, but now is rapidly coming to mean no more than that a person is telephone-literate).

The implications are enormous, but let's just stay focused on sexuality. What I'm attempting to do with this book by allowing my readers access to the secret life of men through their sexual fantasies is precisely what cyberspace is capable of accomplishing. Spontaneously, men are taking to this new medium of communication to express themselves sexually to a degree that they couldn't or wouldn't attempt in the past.

It seems like every online commercial computer network has a human sexuality forum, where users exchange information and ideas. Most of them have "libraries" full of erotic stories, fantasies, tips and personal experiences authored by ordinary men and women whose only credentials are that they, in fact, are ordinary men and women.

When I started the "men's beat" for NBC's *Today Show* more than ten years ago, my plan was to go behind the lines and find out what women—and other men—really needed to know about men. The assumption was that a spy was needed because men weren't willing or able to reveal important aspects of themselves. I couldn't have imagined back then that within a decade or so, men would be eagerly telling strangers all about their wildest fantasies from the comfort of their homes and offices via a computer keyboard.

It's a remarkable breakthrough. As far as I'm concerned the more communication the better. While there are abuses and negatives—all of which seem to be fixable without creating a cyberspace vice squad— at this juncture, cybersex seems to have a lot going for it. I asked more than a dozen men for permission to use their cyberspace fantasies, but my *litspace* is limited and there's only enough for four examples. But they are enough to demonstrate that cyberspace is a sensual and revealing place.

Making Friends

This fantasy from "Mac," like many that are available in cyberspace, is more detailed and elaborate than most of those offered to us in face-to-face interviews, in questionnaires and over the phone. It strikes me that these guys are very comfortable with the medium and aren't reluctant to take the time and effort to express themselves fully.

Our tension had been slowly building for a few weeks. My wife, Lu, and I had been exchanging letters and photos with a man we met by responding to a magazine ad. We were considering the realization of a fantasy of having a threesome that we had been talking about for quite a while now. Tonight we were to meet Jack for the first time. This would be a big first for all three of us. Among the things the three of us had in common, other than possibly sharing sex, was a lack of pubic hair. We all shaved routinely. We knew that just the existence of those hairless genitals would be a big turn-on for us tonight and would probably be a major factor in things going a lot further than just dinner and conversation together. We'd all at least want to see each other's genitals. Beyond that nothing was certain, but we had casually talked about the possible sexual activities we might want to do together. It obviously depended on how we all felt when we finally met and got to know each other a little.

Lu and I were both nervous. She was apprehensive, but excited about the prospect of perhaps having sex with two men at the same time. I had fantasized about this, but wondered if feelings of jealousy or feeling left out would spoil everything when the fantasy was replaced by reality. It was bound to be fun for Jack. He had nothing to lose. But for us, there were a lot of things to consider. If it wasn't going to be pleasurable for both of us, then we shouldn't be doing this. But we had both talked about the fantasy a lot, usually while we were making love, and were very excited by it. We agreed that under the right circumstances, it would be extremely exciting to act out.

It was midafternoon and time to start preparing for our big date. I took my shower first and meticulously shaved the little bit of stubble off my genitals and ass and also shaved my legs completely. Being smooth all over is very sensual to me. Lu was next in the shower. She shaved her legs but saved her pussy for me. Still wet, she lay on the bed and spread her legs, knees up, providing full access to her pussy. There wasn't very much to shave, so the visual stimulation of her beautiful bald pussy caused precome to drip constantly from my cock as I removed every trace of stubble and a few curly hairs that she had missed from shaving herself a few days ago.

Lu sighed and moaned a lot during the shaving. The attention her pussy was getting was obviously enjoyable. But she was really thinking about what might happen later that evening, and the moans of pleasure were due to thoughts of the possibility of our new friend Jack ministering to her most intimate parts as I was at the moment. I knew that's what she was thinking about, because she told me.

Hearing that made me feel a little strange initially, but then I started to feel more excited and my tongue went right to the center of her pussy. I softly pressed the flat part of my tongue into her and drew it up, brushing her clit gently. I repeated this several times. Nothing but moans came from Lu. Then she asked if it was all right that she was really thinking about Jack's tongue in her. I answered by forcing my tongue as deeply into her as I could. Then I sucked her clit into my mouth and tickled it rapidly with my tongue. I alternated thrusting my tongue deeply into her vagina and sucking her clit and lips into my mouth. Her moans increased in intensity and soon she was screaming as I continued my frenzied sucking of her lips and clit and then I felt her shuddering in my mouth and getting much wetter as she screamed through a violent orgasm. Her thighs squeezed my head and held it tightly against her pussy for a minute, then she slowly relaxed.

We both rested quietly for a couple of minutes. Then I

felt her warm lips on my cock, which hardened again quickly. Soon I was inside her very wet and relaxed pussy, feeling very close to orgasm. She asked if it would be exciting to me if later that evening Jack's cock was doing what mine was right now. All I could do then was gasp and shudder as my cock exploded with semen inside her. I quickly withdrew and squirted the rest of my semen on her belly, so she could see as well as feel my excitement and pleasure. Both exhausted, we rested, completely relaxed, dozing off briefly.

Then it was time to get dressed, Lu asked if stockings and a garter belt under a short black wrap dress sounded good. She of course knew what my answer would be. We knew that the wrap dress was a little difficult to be modest in, because it had a tendency to open with every movement and expose her legs to at least her upper thigh level. That would be perfect for this evening. Lu asked if I would rub her all over with some scented body lotion so that she could be as appealing as possible to both Jack and me.

I felt a little funny when she said that, but at the same time it felt exciting to me. She lay front side down first and I carefully covered all of her with the lotion. Then she turned over and I started covering all the rest of her with lotion. "Be sure to get the top part of my thighs and around my pussy. I want Jack to enjoy the scent if he gets real close to me," She said. Lu had now figured out that saying that sort of thing was getting to me in such a way as to increase my sexual tension in a strangely pleasurable way. Now that she knew the effect she had on me, she continued talking like that as we both got dressed. I really didn't know what to say in response in words. But I kissed her deeply several times on her mouth and her pussy as we were getting dressed, so she knew very well what that kind of talk was doing to me. I felt like I was really in some sort of dreamlike state and would need little or no wine that evening to be completely intoxicated.

We met Jack in the bar of a nice restaurant and initially all shook hands a little nervously. Then Lu gave him a warm hug and a kiss on the cheek. Jack blushed and seemed a little shy, but smiled and kissed her back. I didn't feel jealous, but I did feel a little weird. I felt nervous and a little uncomfortable. It was not a foregone conclusion that we would all have sex together that night, but I was fully aware that if we all got along well, it was probably inevitable. We were led to a cozy corner booth and Lu said she wanted to sit between us. I expected that. Jack slid into the booth first and then Lu. It was impossible for her to slide in without the dress unwrapping briefly up to waist level. She pulled it back into position, after she knew that both Jack and I had gotten a good look at her stockings, thighs and black panties. I was actually surprised to see that she wore panties tonight.

The ordering of the wine and the food and the serving of it seemed almost incidental to the small talk we engaged in as we casually shared our interests and personality traits with Jack. We were much more interested in each other. During our conversation Lu and I would touch various parts of each other's bodies somewhat incidentally, but intentionally as we would normally do on a romantic dinner date. I quickly realized that Lu and Jack were also touching, in fact a whole lot.

I wasn't getting nearly as much attention as he was, even though my hands were busy either rubbing her legs or feeling her crotch or caressing the back of her neck, with occasional diversions to her breasts. It was a good thing the restaurant was dimly lit, or I'm sure they would have thrown us out by then. Lu turned toward me and kissed me deeply. Her face was already pretty wet and it became obvious she had been French kissing Jack. She asked if it was okay and I said yes. She was happy to hear that and said that she was having a very good time and felt very comfortable with Jack. I excused myself for a brief trip to the men's room.

When I returned to the table I discovered how comfortable she had really become. Rolled up next to my plate was her pair of panties. I could feel my cock start to react to the situation. She looked at me and smiled and again kissed me and shoved her hand down into my underwear and grabbed my cock. She rubbed her finger over the head of my very wet cock and brought it out, wet her lips with it and kissed me again.

"I want Jack to fuck me," she said, "and I want you right there with me when we do it. Is that all right with you?" I was shocked but I was also getting more and more excited, so I answered by reaching down and feeling her very wet bare pussy and whispered a quiet yes in her ear. She turned back to Jack and kissed him, and although I could feel her body close to mine, both her hands went back to Jack. I felt very strange, but it was an exciting feeling. Lu checked back with me several times to insure that I was okay with what was happening. I was glad she did, because I needed that interaction. If I had started to feel left out, that would have spoiled things for all of us. Lu seemed to know that. Each time I was more okay than the time before. Jack was getting almost all of her attention and his hands were all over her.

It was obvious that Lu was extremely turned on and so was I. Lu turned to me again and smoothed a wet slippery substance from her finger across my lips and kissed me with an open mouth and probing tongue. She had done that before in our lovemaking, and since she hadn't just put her finger in her mouth, I assumed it was from her wet pussy. Then she kissed my ear and whispered passionately, "My finger didn't just come from my pussy! Jack's cock is just as wet and slippery as yours. Why don't we all go to our house now?"

It was a short drive home from the restaurant. Lu played with or sucked on my cock most of the way. Jack followed behind in his own car. When we got home, no one was at all interested in the hot tub. We were too far gone for that. No one said anything of consequence. We just walked into the bedroom and got undressed. We were all anxious about exactly what to do next, but we knew we wanted to do things that we couldn't have done in the restaurant. We all lay down on the bed with Lu in the middle. For a few minutes we examined and admired all the shaved genitals and then massaged each other's "private parts."

Both Jack and I were reluctant to touch each other, but Lu made it clear that she would really love to see us touching and that it would excite her tremendously. Needless to say, her influence was successful. In the interest of sexual exploration and our current level of excitement a little touching seemed okay. Jack and I enjoyed what seemed like several minutes of fondling and exploring each other's shaved genitals. Lu could tell that we both enjoyed it. Now that Jack and I had made each other hard, Lu wanted us to both start paying attention to her.

Lu was delirious with pleasure with all the attention she was getting. Hands and mouths all over her. She gave most of her attention to Jack. She was more excited by the prospect of having Jack than me. While frequently checking to see if I was okay with everything, she realized that I was really getting excited by and getting pleasure from watching her and Jack together. I wasn't sure ahead of time that I would feel that way, but now that it was happening it was a fantastically pleasurable experience. The pleasure was enhanced by Lu's frequent, although brief, caresses and kisses for me, in between the longer and more active kissing and fondling with Jack.

Lu frequently expressed delight at how great it was to be able to play with two hard cocks at the same time. She kept one hand on my cock most of the time, but was much more actively sucking on Jack's cock while he was eating her pussy. I was in an excited trance watching them. At one point they slowed down and relaxed a little, still kissing, though, and feeling each other all over. I would get an occasional deep kiss from Lu and a squeeze on my cock. Both Jack and I started to get a little soft. I heard an almost audible sigh from Lu. I knew her preference was to see and feel hard erections. I knew from her sigh that she hoped they'd both be hard again soon.

Even now I don't know why I did it, but I reached for a lotion dispenser at the side of the bed and squeezed a good amount into my hand. Without asking, I smoothed the lotion onto Jack's hairless cock and balls with both hands. I don't know how I could do such a thing. It just seemed that under those circumstances it was okay. Lu said, Oh, my God! I don't believe my eyes! Oh, but please keep doing it!

Jack got hard very quickly. She kissed me with a very wet mouth and played with my cock and balls excitedly. Then she sucked on my ear and in a passionate and breathy voice in my ear kept encouraging me to do more with Jack and rub the lotion all over his hairless genitals and ass. "You know that feels good when I do that to you, now I want you to do it to him." I could hardly believe what she was telling me. Momentary flashes in my mind told me I shouldn't be doing this. Lu got even more excited and kept kissing me and playing with my cock and saying how exciting it was to her to see me playing with his cock and feeling his prostate deep inside his ass with my finger. "Make him work for me. Make him ready to fuck me," she said. I couldn't believe she was saying that.

She kept talking like that in between wet kisses and sticking her wet tongue in my ear. Both her hands were active on my cock and balls, while my hands were on Jack. "Keep him hard for me, but don't let him come. I want him to come inside me," she said. That was all I could take. I came and squirted semen all over her and roared in orgasmic delight. Lu laughed and said, "Oh, wow, I really love this."

With me completely spent, my hands fell away from Jack's slippery hard cock and lotion-filled asshole. Lu lay back on the bed and spread her legs.

"Now grab his cock and stick it in me," she said. "Stick it in me and tell him to fuck me."

Jack needed very little persuasion. I did as Lu said and held his cock and balls and helped to insert him into Lu's pussy. "I didn't hear you tell him to fuck me yet," she said.

She was right, of course. I had become speechless. "Tell him," she said. "Tell him! Tell him!"

As I continued to massage his balls and asshole while he was pumping up and down in Lu's pussy, I finally got the words out. Instantly they both exploded, Lu screaming and Jack groaning. It was soon over. We were all completely spent and no one could talk except for an occasional moan or sigh. Wet and exhausted we dozed off, still not really sure whether it had really happened or had just been a very exciting fantasy.

Pool Shark

"Dean" is fifty-seven years old and lives in Frederick, Maryland. He is a social worker.

I hate gyms but I do need exercise to stay in shape. So I decided to go swimming twice a week at our public pool.

One day, I saw her. She was wearing a bright orange swimsuit, which matched perfectly with her tanned skin and her long, dark brown hair. I made sure I swam in the same lane she was in. She was doing the backstroke and couldn't see what I was up to. I headed right in her direction, and about two yards before we met, I changed into the backstroke myself. Of course, we bumped.

I pretended to be very angry, and she apologized a thousand times, not calming me down at all. I told her that she would have to pay dearly for this accident. Suddenly, she smiled seductively and said just one word: "How?"

This was going better that I had hoped for, better, in fact, than I was prepared for. I pretended to think for a few seconds before saying: "Would you do whatever I tell you to do for the next twenty-four hours?" She said that was asking a bit much. I wanted to own her for twenty-four hours, she wanted the right to own me for twenty-four hours. Besides, she had to attend classes the next morning. Instead, we decided that she would be mine for the whole upcoming weekend.

She had one more condition. While I owned her, I had to wear a chastity belt, and she would keep the key during that time. Before we parted she told me her name was Rebecca, and she gave me her phone number and address, but I told her to come to my house. I'd call her later that day and give her a list of things to bring.

Finally, Friday night arrived and so did she, carrying a beach bag and wearing a very short white blouse and a jeans skirt that went down to her ankles. Between the skirt and blouse, you could see at least three inches of that beautiful skin.

First, I told her to take off the blouse, but she refused and reminded me that I had to wear a chastity belt myself. She had brought a gorgeous belt for me with a tiny lock that she fastened after helping me into the belt. Only after the belt was in place did she take off her blouse. She was gorgeous, standing there, topless in her long skirt and sandals. I asked her to take off her skirt and panties as well. It was amazing how natural it seemed for her to remove all her clothes in front of a man who was virtually a complete stranger.

When Rebecca was completely naked, I handed her a chastity belt to wear for the rest of the night. The idea was that my key was to be attached to her belt, and her key would be attached to my belt. I had also told her to bring that same swimsuit with her, and now I told her to put it on. It was cut so deep that you could see almost all of her back. Then I took a length of rope and tied her knees together tightly.

There was a D-ring attached to the back of her chastity belt, and I reached into the suit to attach two one-foot chains to it. The chains were very thin, they almost looked like jewelry, but they were very strong. I also attached another, much thicker, chain about three feet long to the same ring. I wouldn't need any of them now, so I dropped the chains into the suit, hidden from sight.

Finally, I allowed her to wear her long skirt again, but no shoes.

It was still very early on this warm summer night, and I decided to go out and have dinner at some fast-food place where they didn't care too much about proper attire, before going to see a movie.

We live in New York, so it was only natural to go to Broadway and show her off. We took the subway. She had some problems walking through the gate with her tied knees, but she managed.

Once we got off the train, we headed for the nearest pizza place. Once we ordered the food and found a table, she discovered that she couldn't sit down—the chain in her back was too painful. I said, "Okay, I'll take out the chains, but only if I may use them." Dutifully, Rebecca lowered her wrists for me to attach the thin chains, and I told her to sit on my lap because I now had to feed her.

I also took the third chain and connected it to one of the belt loops in my jeans to keep her from running away.

We finished our pizza and went to the cinema. I did not release any of the chains, so she had to walk in front of me. I put my head on her shoulder and clasped my hands in front of her belly. We looked like just another flirting couple to anybody but the most careful observer—and who ever pays attention to anybody in New York?

Ordinarily, we would have had plenty of time to get to the movie, but with her hobbled knees, it was clear we couldn't make it. So I grabbed her around the waist and carried her for two or three blocks, but then I found out I couldn't do it anymore and decided to take a cab. We must have looked kind of funny to the driver, clinging together like that, and she in her bare feet and not wearing more than a swimsuit and skirt. I can almost imagine him telling his wife about the strange people he sometimes has to transport! But he took us to the theater on time, and that was all we cared about.

We had to wait in line for half an hour for the tickets, and she surprised me by turning around and giving me a big kiss. Everybody could now see the chain connecting us! Well, we had lots of fun that night, and I don't even remember which movie we saw.

Job Hunting

"Dmitri" is from Valley Forge, Pennsylvania. He works in his father's flower shop and is married, with one child. He told us: "I'm a thirty-five-year-old white male and have a very rich imagination when it comes to sexual fantasies. Even as a young teenager, I had an extremely fertile imagination when it came to creating new scenarios to masturbate by. This has only added to my real-life sexual experiences. One of my favorites is the "Interview."

I enter a very plush business office for a job interview and am greeted by a sophisticated, tall, black woman dressed in a business suit consisting of a jacket and skirt. The interview starts normally enough but soon the questions become more and more personal and of a sexual nature. In my fantasy we speak in very blunt language.

"How large is your cock," she asks. I am deeply embarrassed by the question but feel myself getting aroused. She continues to ask me questions. "How often do you masturbate? Do you enjoy fucking women up the ass? Men?"

I answer all of her questions honestly and completely. At

this point, I've pulled my cock out of my pants and I am openly stroking it in front of her. She sees this but continues to hold a very businesslike approach to the whole thing.

"I want you to come over here and stick your cock in my mouth," she demands, and this I obligingly do. At this point, I come in torrents into her mouth as she moans and swallows every drop.

The Doctor-Patient Relationship

"Evan" is twenty-three and divorced. He lives in Fall River, Massachusetts.

I go to the doctor for a physical. Instead of my usual male doc, there's a beautiful young intern. She goes over me, then it's time for the hernia check. "What do we have here?" she coos, smiling broadly. As I begin to get noticeably excited, she hops up on the exam table and begins fellatio. Then she gets down, pulls her tight little skirt off—no panties—and gets back on the table.

Then she hikes her white coat up and tells me—I'm still naked from the physical—to move up behind her. I enter her, oh so slowly, with the tip of my member. I just hold it there, not thrusting at all, but stroking her hips and legs.

Finally, she screams, "Do me now!" and begins thrusting violently backward. After several hot minutes, she flips over on her back, grabs her calves, and spreads wide. As I pump she reaches around and tickles my scrotum.

I feel my orgasm building from the very core of my being.

As I continue to stroke rapidly, the pressure becomes intense. Then she screams and begins to convulse. As her vaginal walls contract violently around my throbbing penis, I release my orgasm, pumping what seems like gallons of juice into her.

I collapse on top of her. We're both gasping for air and shaking all over. Just as we start to recover a bit, a nurse knocks, then without waiting for a response, enters the room. She looks startled for a moment, then smiles coyly and begins to unbutton her blouse. . . .

One of the things I particularly like about cyberspace is that it can function as a worldwide support group. With a minimum of fuss, you can go online and find other people with similar interests and experiences. Next to the real thing—real people in a real support group in a real community—I can't think of a better way to break out of the sense of isolation and loneliness that can be so dispiriting.

Part of the attraction—and danger—of cyberspace is that it offers human contact without human contact. By preserving anonymity, online computer networks encourage users to engage with each other while maintaining their detachment. The risks of rejection and ridicule aren't quite as high as they would be in face-to-face encounters.

This feature is powerfully appealing. It seems to be an antidote to the poison that has always tainted human discourse and relationships—fear. If I can "tell all" to a computer pen pal whom I've never met and discover that I'm not sick or disgusting, it is an invaluable service.

Would a face-to-face exchange be better? Probably, in that it would demonstrate that our fears of "being found out" and rejected are overblown and groundless. But if those human exchanges aren't taking place now, for whatever reason, I'd rather have it happen in cyberspace than not at all. Establishing communication between men and women, women and women, men and men may lead eventually to deep and rich exchanges without technology acting as the go-between. It's a start in that direction.

This book has been all about communication. Despite our modern ways and sophistication—our media savvy and computer smarts—we are not very good at it. The simple act of telling another human being what we want and why we want it remains excruciatingly difficult. As for telling ourselves—that's where the problem starts.

Like all skills, communication is learned. Anthropologists say that humans have a very long developmental stage compared to other creatures because we have so much to learn in order to survive. But for some reason, the curriculum has been woefully inadequate when it comes to communication, and almost nonexistent in terms of sexual communications.

Maybe there's an evolutionary reason for that: Those who talked about it didn't do it and therefore didn't thrive as well as those who did. But if that were the case, we'd probably all be growling at each other and pointing at our genitals.

No, seriously, I think the sexual communication gap is cultural and it must be bridged. The only way to do that is to *learn* the skill of conveying important knowledge to another human being. Notice I said *knowledge,* not information. There's a difference. Facts are information, but without the necessary ingredients—the nuances, the shading, the texture—to make them meaningful or useful. Mostly, the missing ingredient is emotion. We tell people things but they never learn how important those things really are. How could they? We didn't include that part.

We've been trained to guard our emotions and to hold them in check. This makes for a more orderly and businesslike society, but hasn't done much for our sex lives. Sexuality is the realm of emotions.

Without them, sex is barren and cold. Emotional reticence, combined with the culturally mandated reluctance to talk about sex, has made many of us woefully inarticulate.

When it comes to learning sexual communication skills, few of us have proper role models. Many of our parents could barely bring themselves to stutter out the facts of life to us during adolescence. Our siblings and friends are in the same boat.

In loving relationships, where emotion and communication should flourish, two sets of sexual communication dysfunctions can instead reinforce each other, producing the classic formula familiar to every marriage counselor: "I talk, he listens, we don't understand each other."

One of the things I was proudest of about my show, *Real Personal,* was that it served as a global town meeting on the subject of human sexuality. While lots of valuable information and knowledge is exchanged, there's an even greater benefit in exposing millions of people to the process of sexual communication. We're teaching that essential skill night after night. People are learning that they can talk about the subject without fear.

This book is doing what *Real Personal* couldn't do. It's offering you an opportunity to delve into areas that are too supercharged and intense even for today's "anything goes" broadcasting climate. Sex is still "not ready for prime time" on most TV networks and cable channels or prime shelf space in bookstores, unless it's suitably disguised as trashy entertainment. Yet, sex is abundantly available in real time and in real life; it won't go away. We *have* to make sense of it. Either we learn to share our secret lives or go on living, in the words of Henry David Thoreau, "lives of quiet desperation."